Social Media Marketing
for Beginners

Turn Your Business into a Cash Cow
using Tiktok, Facebook, and
Instagram - A Complete Digital
Marketing
Guide Included

By John Shackelford

The following Book is reproduced below with the goal of providing information that is as accurate and reliable as possible. Regardless, purchasing this Book can be seen as consent to the fact that both the publisher and the author of this book are in no way experts on the topics discussed within and that any recommendations or suggestions that are made herein are for entertainment purposes only. Professionals should be consulted as needed prior to undertaking any of the action endorsed herein. This declaration is deemed fair and valid by both the American Bar Association and the Committee of Publishers Association and is legally binding throughout the United States. Furthermore, the transmission, duplication, or reproduction of any of the following work including specific information will be considered an illegal act irrespective of if it is done electronically or in print. This extends to creating a secondary or tertiary copy of the work or a recorded copy and is only allowed with the express written consent from the Publisher. All additional rights reserved. The information in the following pages is broadly considered a truthful and accurate account of facts and as such, any inattention, use, or misuse of the information in question by the reader will render any resulting actions solely under their purview. There are no scenarios in which the publisher or the original author of this work can be in any fashion deemed liable for any hardship or damages that may befall them after undertaking information described herein.

Additionally, the information in the following pages is intended only for informational purposes and should thus be thought of as universal. As befitting its nature, it is presented without assurance regarding its prolonged validity or interim quality. Trademarks that are mentioned are done without written consent and can in no way be considered an endorsement from the trademark holder.

Table of Contents

Introduction

Social media marketing is one of the main tools businesses have to build brand awareness, promote their products and services, and find new customers. This should not come as a surprise, considering people are spending the majority of their time on TikTok, Instagram, Facebook, Twitter and Youtube. The smartphone has become our best friend and the smartest marketers can take advantage of this circumstance.

However, even if consumers are staring at their phones for several hours every day, most companies and personal brands do not know how to properly use the power of digital marketing to increase their sales. In fact, oftentimes the entirety of their digital marketing strategy is based on just posting random content on their website, hoping to get some organic traffic and sales.

This used to work in 2019 and 2020. However, things change pretty rapidly these days.

The bad news is that this approach does not work anymore. In fact, with the digitization of more and more companies, the internet is becoming a crowded space and you need a clear strategy to defeat your competitors. The good news is that not a lot of businesses and solopreneurs have made the switch to a more programmatic and systematic approach to digital marketing yet. This gives a big advantage to those that are willing to put in the work now and build a strong and solid online presence for their company or personal brand.

In this book, you will discover everything there is to know about an effective and powerful social media marketing strategy. From the basic concepts, like identifying the target audience and creating an effective editorial plan, to the more advanced tactics, each step of the way will be presented with a clear goal in mind: monetization.

After all, the ability to actually convert users into clients is what distinguishes a good digital marketer from a wannabe entrepreneur. The first one is focused on generating revenues for his company or for himself if he is building a personal brand. The second one, instead, believes that likes and comments will help him pay his bills. You have to decide in which category you want to belong to, but we can assure that everything is much easier for your business when you are able to generate paying customers like clockwork.

That is why we decided to write this book. We had enough of all the "Gurus" out there that are selling you expensive books and programs with the promise to teach you their "special tactic". The reality is that there is not a secret to social media marketing. Everything has already been said time and time again and you just need to put in a good amount of work.

However, nobody has ever put together a book that goes into the little details of every aspect of this fascinating world. We wanted to do just that, leaving nothing on the table. Every information you need to turn your social media presence into an effective and lasting money making machine is contained in this book.

We are happy to have you on board with us for this amazing journey, we are sure you will learn a lot.

To your success!

Chapter 1

A Basic Introduction to Social Media Marketing

Before getting started with the most effective strategies you can use to market your products or services using social media, we think it is important to give a clear and concise definition of what we are talking about. The risk, in fact, is to label every marketing activity conducted online as social media marketing. This could not be farther from the truth, as you will better understand reading this book.

To better define what social media marketing is, we can use the definition from Wikipedia.

Social media marketing is the branch of marketing that deals with generating visibility on social media, virtual communities and aggregators 2.0 for companies, public entities, associations and personal brands.

One of the characteristics that affect today's communication is precisely the impossibility of creating face-to-face relationships with your users or rather with your audience.

As you can see by the definition, there is no social media marketing without someone to market to. We call these people the target audience or simply audience.

The target audience refers to a group of potential customers to whom a company wants to sell its products or services. It is highly important to create a well balanced relationship with the people you want to address and, to do so, you need to interact with them. Social media offer the perfect vehicle to do that in a simple and effective way. This is why more and more companies are relying on the power of these platforms to interact with their audience.

Therefore, we can use a more simplistic definition of social media marketing, but that will assure us to get to the point. Here is the definition we will use during the course of this book.

The purpose of social media marketing is to create a conversation with users.

And what about the good old website? Many think that social media marketing is separate from blogging, as they are two different forms of communication. However, it is not completely true.

The truth lies in between, in the sense that objectively the communicative style must necessarily be different. It is true that the target is always the same, but it is also equally true that those who interact with the company through social media do not want long and complicated posts to read. However, it is also very true that those who read a blog may not be interested in scrolling pictures on Instagram or liking posts on Facebook. Hence why it is always important to have a clear idea of "where" we are communicating, not only who we are talking to.

It is important to go a little bit deeper here and point out that it is not only a matter of blogs or social platforms. The difference lies in between the various social media as well.

This means that each social network wants its specific type of communication and, therefore, there is a further differentiation of the work to be done. We will get a better grasp of this concept when we will talk about the different platforms specifically.

Returning to the great help that social platforms such as Facebook, Instagram or Linkedin can give to companies and personal brands in their marketing efforts, what we must focus on to understand is what it means to invest in social media marketing activities. In fact, some people still take it lightly and think that posting random pictures on Instagram or spamming comments on Facebook pages is what this is all about. On the contrary, social media marketing needs to be taken very seriously as it can really help a company or a brand a lot in terms of engagement and sales.

Putting it in practice

Now we can really dive into the subject and understand what it really means to invest in a social media marketing activity.

by someone with experience or at least by someone that understands the concepts we have just talked about. In particular, a good social media marketer should be able to do the following things.

- **Make a detailed analysis of the communication type and the target audience**. This is absolutely critical, as we will see in the chapter dedicated to the creation of the potential buyer identity.

- **Know the social and web marketing communication dynamics**. By this we mean he should be able to understand how to properly write on the different platforms and how to adapt the same message to various types of posts.

- **Have a certain versatility in the use of graphics programs such as Canva, Photoshop and Gimp.** Big brands and companies might have the possibility to outsource this part. However, if you are just starting an online business or need to develop your personal brand, having some basic knowledge of graphic design is fundamental.

- **Have the ability to write in a persuasive way**. We are talking about copywriting, which is the skill that allows social media marketers to persuade people to perform a certain activity using just written words. It is obviously a very important skill to turn followers into paying customers.

- **Be a great moderator.** Managing comments and feedback requires great skills and an emotionless approach. A good social media marketer knows how to not be overwhelmed by what other people say, yet taking their opinion into consideration.

- **Use tools effectively.** Social automation is essential and nowadays there are endless tools that can help the social media marketer to save time and be more effective. Using these tools in the correct way is very important for long lasting success.

As you can see, there are many skills someone needs to develop to become a good social media marketer. This is why some companies decide to hire a social media manager that knows how to manage their campaigns for them.

Even if this is a positive trend and more and more brands are starting to realize the importance of being decisive in their communication, there is still a lot of work to do. In fact, most companies still believe that in order to communicate on social media is enough to post simple photos or videos. It is clear they do not have the right knowledge.

The starting point is the data and here, in fact, the social media manager intervenes. Anyone who carries out this work knows very well that before creating a social media marketing plan, enough time is needed to devote to the analysis of the target and competitors. a competitor in the following way.

A competitor is a company or personal brand in the same or a similar niche that offers a similar product or service.

Furthermore, another erroneous belief is that concerning the presumption of knowing immediately how it is best to communicate with your audience. To really understand what works, you have to experiment and test everything extensively.

This is why the social media manager is an expert in all social platforms, knows their potential and is able to integrate them effectively with each other, thus carrying out a skilled social media marketing activity.

Now that we have specified what this work consists of, let's focus for a moment on what the benefits of social media marketing can be for your business. An entire book could not summarize the great returns a good social media marketing strategy can yield, but we can try to give you an overview. If you decide to focus on social media marketing in a serious way, you will get the following opportunities.

- You will have the opportunity to greatly improve the relationship with your target audience, as you will always keep them updated on the news of your company.

- You will be able to catch your audience's attention much more easily.

- You will improve your personal branding skills. It is useless to lie, to be actively present on social media, it helps your brand a lot. By the way, for the newcomers, a brand is an identification symbol, trademark, logo, name, word or phrase that companies use to distinguish their product from others.

- You can take advantage of social media marketing activities to increase traffic to your site or your blog, depending on the goal you want to achieve.

- You will be able to maintain relationships with your customer, also trying to investigate his satisfaction with your product or service. This means you will be able to get constant feedback on what you are providing, which could be a great tool to revise your offer even on a monthly basis.

- You will be able to start establishing yourself as an expert or leader in your niche, always sharing updated content regarding your work and that of your company. This is called brand awareness and we believe it is the greatest thing social media marketing can give you.

- You can increase the chance that your offer will be seen by your potential customer. You can do this using what is known as "organic traffic" or paid advertising. We believe that a combination of the two is a great resource to put your offer at the centre of your niche. Do not worry, we are going to cover both traffic sources in the coming chapters.

As mentioned before, these are only a few of the advantages that social media marketing can give to those that are willing to take the risk to expose their company or personal brand online. However, as you might have understood by now, we feel that it is much more risky to leave your competitors free to saturate each social media with their content and offers, than it is to take the chance and develop a social media marketing strategy.

In fact, in today's world everything is done digitally and users' attention has become a currency that each company and personal brand should try to earn. Think about it, when was the last time you made a purchase based on a billboard you saw down the road? Now think again and try to remind yourself when was the last time you bought something online.

are becoming more and more digital as time goes on. As an entrepreneur or influencer it is your duty to take advantage of this opportunity and monetize your online presence as much as possible.
In the next chapters we are going to tell you exactly how to do it.

Chapter 2

How to Identify Your Target Audience

As mentioned in the previous chapter, the first thing to do when developing a social media marketing strategy is to identify the target audience.

Who are we talking to?

It is such a basic question but that it is not always easy to answer. In this chapter we are going to give you some practical tips and ideas on how to identify your audience in a precise and effective way.

Now that you know why a target audience is essential, it's time to select your first audience group. Below is a list of features you should identify.

1. Demographics

Demographics are the criteria that you use to describe a specific part of the population. Some examples of demographics are:

- Age
- Kind
- Income
- Marital status
- Occupation
- Educational level

2. Location

You can also narrow your audience based on geography or location. You can select a district, city, province or country. You can also specify your audience by distance. For example, you can target customers within a 10-mile radius of your city. Or you can target customers within your city and the cities around it.

For those who want to start an online business for customers or clients around the world, it may not be necessary to set a specific distance. Still, it is possible that as your business grows, you will see certain cities or countries where most of your customers tend to come from. You can specifically target those areas later or move on to other locations that can bring you the opportunities you want.

3. Psychographic

Unlike demographics, a group's psychographics are more difficult to guess externally, as these are more relevant to their personality. Here are some audience psychographics, which you can specify.

- Board game fans
- Frequent backpackers
- Beginning gardeners
- Stamp collectors

You can also specify what the ideal audience believes about a topic or problem. For example:

- People who appreciate video games developed by independent developers rather than large corporate development.

- People who are concerned about the environment or climate change.
- People who believe conciliation is essential.
- People who are always looking for the lowest price.

4. Choose at least two identifiers

While it is not necessary to identify all of the above characteristics, it is necessary to know at least two of them. Why two? Having a single criterion will leave you with a very large market. On the other hand, compiling all features may leave you with a too narrow market. It might also help you review the examples listed earlier in this chapter. See if you can find the demographic, location and psychographic identifiers used in each audience group.

Marketing tools for your target audience

Even after following the steps above and copying the spreadsheet, you might not feel confident about your selected audience. If you need to help understand your target audience and learn more about them, the following tools can be helpful.

1. Facebook Insights

Facebook Insights Audience is a tool that allows you to specify and learn more about your target audience. Start by selecting different audience criteria such as location, age, interests and behaviors. Then, you will be able to know more about them, including the size of your target market and any trends in demographics or psychographics.

Let's say you want to open a comic shop in Dallas. You can select "Dallas" for the location and under "Interests", select "Comics". Audience Insights then automatically reveals that Facebook users in Dallas who are interested in comics tend to be in the 25-34 age group. There is also a balance between the male and female members of that target market. Facebook also gives you an estimate for the size of the market: around 100,000 people.

additional demographics and psychographics that you can use to define your audience. It can also give a general estimate of how large that potential audience might be.

One caveat you need to know about the data is that most of it is based on self-reported behavior data on Facebook. This means that you shouldn't treat it as 100% accurate, but it can give you a good big picture idea about your target audience. If your desired audience doesn't really use Facebook, then it might not be useful to you.

2. Google Trends

Google Trends helps you determine interest in a particular keyword or topic over time. This can be useful if you want to narrow down a position for your business idea as well as any general trends.

Let's say you want to open a board game store in the United States. Type in board game related keywords in Google Trends. You can therefore find the best areas, cities and states with the most interest in table games. You will also quickly see that interest in board games is seasonal - constantly peaks mid-November (before Thanksgiving) until Christmas Eve.

This tells you that your target audience tends to be seasonal shoppers, but that there is also some consistent interest in board games over the years.

3. MyBestSegments

Claritas MyBestSegments has two tools that can come in handy when defining your target market, as long as that market is within the US.

ZIP Code Lookup is most useful for businesses that want specific target areas. Just enter a postcode in the form, and it'll list the common marketing segments available for that area. You can also get other demographics breakdowns for the area, such as age, income, household composition, and race and ethnicity.

Don't forget to click on the market segments in the results. This will give you more details on other interests, behaviors and demographics of that segment.

Test Your Target Market

This would also be a good time to start testing your target audience to see if it's a good fit for your product or service you are offering. Here are some ways to do it.

1. Get Feedback from people in your target audience

Do you know some people who might fall into that target audience? If you do, you can talk to them about your business. Show them mockups of your product photos or list the services you intend to offer. Find out what they think. Specifically, find out if they've purchased similar products or services before, what their main concerns were and were satisfied with the experience.

You will know the target audience is a fit for your offering if they seem highly enthusiastic, have bought from similar your business is trying to solve.

If you lack direct leads that fall into your target market, look for online and offline dealing groups. Online groups, you can search for Facebook groups, Reddit Communities or message boards that are relevant to the audience you are targeting. Offline groups could include special interest groups such as Garden Clubs or your local chamber of commerce. You can also take advantage of relevant public events such as conventions or Meetups and ask around.

2. Set up a Mailing List

You can also set up an online mailing list and get subscribers through advertising or posting about it on social media or online groups. If you get several subscribers in a few days, you will know that there is some interest in your offering.

Dan Benjamin, a podcaster and entrepreneur, recently talked about having a shirt designed, uploading a mockup of it, and creating a mailing list template via Tinyletter for hundred people had joined, interested in the shirt. Only after he did it he opened an online shop for it.

Other tools you can use to build your mailing list are MailChimp, Constant Contact, and GetResponse.

3. Create a landing page

Instead of a mailing list, you can also opt for a landing page. In addition to asking people to subscribe to a mailing list, you can also ask them to pre-order, or to get additional information (for example, downloading an ebook or brochure or playing an informative video). The number of people who follow through on the page's main call to action can give you an idea, whether your target audience will respond to your offers or not.

Once you have enough followers, you will be able to see their group demographics. Does it match with your recipients? If it does, then you are on the right track. If it's different, you need to make some changes to your target audience.

It is also possible to use a combination of the above techniques. You could purchase an ad that leads to a landing page. Or you could go for an online group and after getting their feedback, ask interested people to join your mailing list.

When you start acting on your marketing plans, your target audience may change - and that's normal. As you grow your business and by learning more about what works, you will be able to refine your target audience. You might realize that there is a less affluent market that you want to reach. Or you may find that different subgroups within your target audience respond to different product benefits. If your target audience isn't responding the way you want, or if you realize they aren't a good fit for your bids, either adjust your bids or rethink the way you define your target audience.

It is tempting to skip the steps above and proceed with the more aggressive steps like buying Facebook ads or printing flyers. But the foundation of your marketing plan should be who your customers are. How you write the copy, the design choices you make, and where you choose to advertise all depend on the needs and interests of the target audience. Once you have a clear picture of who your target is, it will be a lot easier to come up with the rest of your social media marketing plan. Whatever you do, please remember this, as it is extremely important.

Questions you can ask yourself to determine the target audience

Marketing and sales should work together in gathering key information about the target audience. In particular, it is useful to answer some basic questions as we have seen at the beginning of this chapter. Here are some more detailed questions you might want to ask yourself to have a much clearer picture of who you would like to sell your product or service to.

- What are their most urgent problems? Are they worried about not having enough money? Do they worry about their health?

- What is their typical working day like? Do they have a job or are they self employed?

- What is their decision making process based on? Do they value word of mouth more than advertising or is it the other way around?

- What are their reasons for purchasing a product or service? What problems are they trying to solve?

- What information do they need at each stage of the buying cycle to feel comfortable? Do they need to be followed each step of the way or do they prefer not to be pressured at all?

- Where do they get information about the problem they are trying to solve? Which platforms do they use the most?

- Who do they consult with for advice? Do they get advice from a professional or do they value the opinion of the average Joe?

- What terms do they use to describe their challenges and goals? Are they excited about the problems they are trying to solve or is it something they just want to be done with?

- What are their characteristic traits in terms of purchasing behavior? Do they tend to make impulsive decisions or do they think about it for a long time before pressing the buy button?

- What are their distinctive demographics? Are they men or women? Are they married and does this matter to your offer?

And the list could go on forever. Just do not be paralized by these questions and do not worry if you are not able to answer them all. When it comes to identifying your target audience, enough is enough and only by testing you can actually find out what works and what does not. Social media marketing needs to be done in practical terms, not just in your mind. Do not forget this as it can make or break your success.

Chapter 3

The 6 Steps Social Media Marketing Plan

Now that we have discovered who we are talking to, it is important to lay out a powerful plan to interact with them in the most effective way possible. Here is where the social media marketing plan comes into play.

In this chapter, we are going to discuss the 6 steps involved with the creation of every social media marketing plan that aims at turning viewers' attention into sales. Let's get started.

What is a Social Media Marketing plan?

A social media marketing plan is the summary of all the actions you intend to take and the goals you want to achieve for your business through the use of social media marketing. That plan should include a review of the current status of your profiles, the goals you want to achieve for each one of them, and the tools you intend to use for this purpose.

In general, the more specific you can be in defining the plan, the more effective you will be in its implementation. Try to be concise and don't make your social media marketing strategy so overwhelming that it becomes impossible to execute. The plan must guide your actions, but it must also serve as a unit of measure by which to determine whether or not you are succeeding on social media. You certainly don't want to do it yourself from the start and we suggest you hire a social media manager to do that. In case you do not have the financial resources to delegate this at first, we recommend you follow the following six steps.

Step 1 - Set SMART goals to achieve

The first step in any social media marketing strategy is to establish the goals and results you want to achieve. Setting these goals also allows you to react quickly when social media campaigns aren't meeting your expectations. Without setting any goals, you don't have the means to evaluate your performance or to demonstrate the ROI of your efforts.

The goals you set should be in line with your general marketing strategy, to ensure that the activity on social networks is always oriented towards the same purposes. With an effective social media marketing strategy capable of advancing the business, it will be easier for those who follow you to decide to buy your products or invest in you. Instead of aiming for purely aesthetic goals, such as the number of "likes" or shares on Instagram, it would be better to focus on more advanced measures, such as the number of customers obtained, the opinions raised or the amount of traffic on your site. Always try to set specific, measurable, achievable, relevant goals with a well-defined time limit.

The simplest way to start a social media marketing plan is to set at least three goals. Always evaluate very well what the result of a given goal will be and based on the latter to keep track of your progress in that direction.

We like to use the SMART method to set goals for our businesses. Here is what smart stands for.

- **Specific**. Your goal must be specific in terms of numbers and methods you decide to use. "Gaining more followers" is not specific, "Gaining 100 followers on Instagram using paid ads" is much better.

- **Measurable**. You have to be able to measure your progress towards your goals. In fact, it is impossible to know if you are doing the right things if you do not have a proper way to measure your progress. Using specific numbers is useful in this case as well.

- **Achievable**. Your goals should be challenging but achievable. In fact, studies have shown that we are able to push ourselves if the task at hand is difficult but not impossible to achieve based on where we are on a specific point in time. For instance, if you are just starting out you cannot set your goal to be to reach one million followers, as it is way too unrealistic.

Start small and build your confidence over time.

- **Relevant**. Your goal should be relevant to your mission. That is why it is so important to have a clear vision for your company or personal brand, before setting goals. You need to know if what you are doing is aligning with who you want to be or not. Make sure that it does, because it makes all the difference.

- **Time effective**. You cannot have an unlimited amount of time to reach your goals, because in this way you will never accomplish anything. Try to set specific deadlines in the future for your goals and you will see how easier it will be for you to achieve them.

Here is an example of an effective goal set using the SMART method.

"We will get 500 followers on Instagram by the end of this month using paid advertising on our most performing posts and posting twice a day each day of the week".

We hope you are able to see how clear this goal is and how it paves the road to its accomplishment.

Phase 2 - Evaluate where you are right now

Before establishing your social media marketing plan, however, you need to evaluate what use you have made of social media so far and what results you have achieved. Try to understand what kind of users follow you on social networks and which social platforms your potential audience uses, then compare your social activity with that of your competition.

Once the evaluation process is complete, you should have a clearer idea of how many and which social accounts represent your business, who manages them and what their purpose is. This evaluation must always be kept up to date, especially if your business is growing.

It should also be clear which accounts need to be updated and which ones should be deleted altogether. Reporting fraudulent accounts serves to make sure that people looking for you online only connect to the official accounts of the brand you manage and messages that you approve.

An important part of your social media marketing plan is creating a "mission" for each social profile. These statements of intent will help you focus your attention on a very specific goal that you want to achieve using Facebook, Twitter or any other social network. They will guide your actions and help you get back on track when these profiles become less effective. Plus, they force you to realize that not all social networks are good for everything. Instagram can be perfect for driving sales of a clothing brand, but for a construction supply company Facebook might be the best choice. Take the time to define the purpose of each social profile you have. If you can't imagine the purpose of a profile then you should probably delete it.

An example of a well written mission is the following. We use Instagram to advertise our company's values and attract new talents". We hope you can see how clear it is and how much confidence it provides to the audience and to the company.

To write missions in the best way, you need to know the audience of each of your profiles in an in-depth way. By analyzing the habits of your customers you will get a clear point of view on the position occupied by each of your social media profiles towards your customers.

Phase 3 - Create or improve your social media accounts

After evaluating your accounts, it's time to work on your online presence. Choose the most suitable social networks for your company to achieve its goals. If you don't already have an active profile for those social networks, create one from scratch, keeping in mind what general purposes you have set for your company or personal brand and what kind of audience you intend to reach. If you already have active accounts, change and update them to get the most out of them.

Each social network has a different audience and should be managed accordingly. Find out how to optimize your profiles to achieve the goals you have set: optimizing your profiles for search engines can bring more web traffic to your site, while promoting your accounts on other social networks can help you increase the reach of the site that you publish your content on. In general, your social profiles should be complete and the images and texts designed specifically for each specific social network.

Phase 4 - Get inspiration from industry leaders, competitors and customers

One of the main reasons for using social networks is that your potential customers are already using them. This is true for your competitors as well. If it seems a little discouraging to know that competition is already here, think that in this way you already have a wealth of knowledge available, to be easily integrated into your social media marketing plan. We advise you to take inspiration from the competition to understand what kind of information and content attracts the attention of users the most. In addition to that, you can use social listening activities to understand how to distinguish yourself from others and reach out to potential customers more effectively.

Finally, consumers can be an additional source of inspiration, not only for the content they share, but also for how they write their messages about your company or your specific niche. Study the style your potential clients use in their tweets and try to imitate it, study their habits, what they share and why, and use these factors to design your social marketing plan.

An additional source of inspiration for your social media marketing plan could be industry leaders. There are giants who exploit social media marketing in an absolutely fantastic way, like Red Bull or Ferrero. In every conceivable sector there are examples of companies that manage to distinguish themselves with advanced and particularly effective social media marketing strategies. Follow them and learn all you can from them. Don't be afraid to do research to find out if they've shared social media ideas or secrets elsewhere on the web.

Here are some brands to be inspired by depending on the niche you are in.

- Content Marketing: Virgin

- Customer support through social media: Tangerine
- Social media advertising: AirBnB
- Facebook strategy: Coca-Cola
- Twitter strategy: Oreo
- Strategy on Instagram: National Geographic

Step 5 - Create a content plan and editorial calendar

Using quality content is key to being successful on social media. Your social marketing plan should include a content marketing plan that includes strategies for creating and managing content and an editorial calendar.

Your content marketing plan should help you answer the following points.

- What kind of content you want to post and promote through social media.
- How often you intend to publish.
- The type of audience expected for each content category.
- Who will be in charge of creating content.
- How you intend to promote what you publish.

An editorial calendar lists the publication dates and times for blog posts, Facebook posts, Instagram posts, and other content you plan to use in your social media marketing campaigns. Create the calendar and then schedule the messages in advance, instead of constantly updating the profiles throughout the day. In any case it is necessary to take care of the language and format of these messages. Spontaneity must be reserved for engagement and customer service.

Make sure your editorial calendar reflects the mission you have assigned to each social profile. For instance, if the goal of your LinkedIn profile is to find new customers, make sure you publish enough content that generates leads. Hootsuite social media executive Jaime Stein recommends establishing a matrix to determine what percentage of a profile to dedicate to different types of posts. Here is an example of how you can split your content.

- 50% of the content is posted on the corporate blog
- 25% of the content must come from other sources, like users or competitors

- 20% of the contents will be used to explain the company mission
- 5% of your content must be about human resources and company culture

If you are not sure how to split your content, you should follow the so-called "Rule of Thirds" of social media marketing. Here is what it states.

- *⅓ of your social content promotes your business, converts readers into customers and generates profits.*
- *⅓ of your social media content must bring out and share ideas and stories from established leaders in your industry or companies similar to yours.*
- *⅓ of your content must be based on personal interactions and the creation of your personal brand.*

We feel that this is an interesting split of the content and that it could yield great results in almost any niche. Therefore, we recommend you to follow this strategy.

Step 6 - Check, evaluate and adapt your social media marketing plan

To know what changes to make to your social media marketing strategy, you need to carry out continuous checks. This means you should periodically test every activity you carry out on social networks; keep track of your links using url abbreviations and utm codes; use Hootsuite's analytics tools to determine the success and reach of each of your campaigns, and use Google Analytics to check which users arrive on your page via social networks. Record and evaluate your successes and failures and modify your social marketing plan accordingly.

Surveys are another important tool for measuring your success. This applies both online and offline. Ask your followers, contacts in your e-mail address list and visitors to your site to give an evaluation of what they see on social media. In fact, oftentimes the direct approach is the most effective one when it comes to gathering feedback. Also address your offline customers, asking if social networks played any role in their decision to purchase your product. Their opinions could prove to be crucial in understanding how to improve your social media marketing strategy. In creating a social media marketing plan, the most important thing is to know that it is something that is bound to change constantly. In fact, new social networks are popping up every day and you may want to add them to your plan; every time you reach a goal, you may decide to change it or find new ones; you may have new challenges to face, or as your business grows, you may need to add roles and increase your social media presence in different branches or countries. In short, it is a constantly evolving situation, so it is necessary to be flexible and ready to adapt. Rewrite your strategy to take advantage of the results of your latest analysis and make sure those who work with you are aware of the changes.

So, by now you should have a clear idea of what a six steps social media marketing plan looks like. In the coming chapters we are going to dive a little deeper and discuss some key elements of your plan.

Chapter 4

Create Your Editorial Plan

Now that we have discussed the importance of having a social media marketing plan, it is time to dive deeper into some of the singular aspects of it. Let's start by taking a look at the editorial plan.

Establishing an editorial plan for your social media marketing plan based on the study of the habits of your target audience and analytical data on traffic and engagement is the best way to make your company's content strategy effective.

The editorial plan must help organize the contents created (on the blog or on the company website) and publish them methodically and consistently, through a publication calendar that covers a sufficiently long period of time to set up a strategy and verify its effectiveness, based on the results obtained. Another benefit brought by the creation of an editorial plan concerns the direct involvement of one's team towards the achievement of a common marketing goal, through collaborative resources that allow to jointly build the business plan.

Social media marketing represents an excellent opportunity to achieve business goals, which can be the acquisition of leads, the increase in traffic to the website, customer loyalty using customer care or, even better, attract potential customers through inbound marketing techniques. Of course, social media marketing is not enough to achieve certain goals. It is necessary to have a strategic web marketing plan to be implemented in order to achieve corporate and profitable results in terms of business.

In order to get started with an editorial plan, it is necessary to have clear corporate goals and establish the roles of the people who will take part in the realization of the project. The briefing between the components of the company is of fundamental importance, in order to have a clear understanding of the actions to be taken. The briefing will define the key elements of communication between the brand and the public. In particular, they will establish the following aspects.

- **Reference sector and principles on which the brand is based on.** In which niche does the company want to position in? What is your company mission?

- What are the products and services offered and what are their main features?

- **Defining the target audience**. An analysis of consumer behaviors and tastes will be fundamental, in order to identify the typical consumer and adapt the tone of voice of the brand and the choice of which social media platform to use.

- **Strengths and weaknesses of the brand.** Strengths must be communicated effectively, while weaknesses must be kept under control to know where problems can develop.

- **Competitor analysis.** Observing competitors is an advantage, it can provide various ideas to take into consideration for your strategy, obviously without copying, but rather to differentiate and innovate.

- **The choice of social channels.** Not all social media platforms are suitable for a company or personal brand. Based on the type of product or service and target audience, a social network will be more suitable than another, taking into account that each social network has its own characteristics and above all a specific target audience.

After this briefing, it is necessary to define at least 5 keywords that represent the brand, so as to have exact references during the subsequent phase of content creation, which the editorial plan will convey through social media in the most effective way possible.

Choosing the right content

According to the trends of 2020, the contents that will acquire more and more consensus among the public are the visual contents. We are mainly talking about videos and images, which get 65% more engagement than textual content, and generate a much higher number of shares.

That is where the success of platforms like Instagram comes from. In fact, it is known that visual content is king on Instagram. Let's never forget to adapt the size of the images to the different social networks. To do this we can use Landscape, the free Sprout Social platform with which to resize the photos you want to publish you like on social media.

The visual content to be included in an editorial plan can be of the following types.

- images;
- photos;
- infographics;
- videos;

- text and images combined;
- screenshots;
- photo collages;
- cartoons;
- quotes and affirmations;
- video tutorial on the use of a product;

It is good that the shared contents are always varied and of different types, so we integrate the visual with informative articles. For example, for effective corporate storytelling, it is good to tell about what happens in the company. You can include the new goals achieved, new partnerships, organized events and directly ask questions to your audience about what type of product they prefer and which one's novelty it expects to see. All of these combined could form a good content for an editorial plan.

The scheduling of contents

Once you have taken into account the audience to be involved and the different types of content to be developed, the time for scheduling has arrived. When planning your content, you need to keep three things in mind. These are the following.

- the choice of days;
- the times of publication;
- the frequency of publication;

To create a quick reference editorial calendar it is best to use an excel document. The days are entered horizontally, from Monday to Sunday, the hours vertically. The choice of times and days on which to build our editorial plan for social media must be decided keeping in mind the characteristics of the target audience.

You can also use Google Calendar if it is a tool that you are familiar with.

As for the US timetables, the reach of an article or image is maximum in the time slot between 8am and 9am in the morning, between 1pm and 4pm in the afternoon, and from 9pm to 10:30pm in the evening. The ideal thing is to reserve a testing period before setting fixed deadlines in the editorial calendar. You have to try different time slots, then choose the ones that have had the most engagement and yield the greatest results.

Regarding the frequency of publication, your editorial plan must consider the type of brand and the social media on which you decide to publish on. Consider for example a brand in the publishing sector. In this case, it is good to publish at least 3 or 4 times a day on Facebook, while on Twitter it must have a much higher frequency such as 20-30 tweets a day.

Now that you have laid out an efficient editorial plan, it is time to start creating effective and engaging content. The next chapter will tell you more about it.

Chapter 5

Create Amazing Content for Your Editorial Plan

Viral or winning content is content that converts. This is simply it. It is when it stimulates people's interest to the point of moving something inside them and therefore increasing the engagement they have with the company that published it. Content can inspire, motivate, educate, inform and turn viewers into paying customers.

It is not a secret that in this book we focus mainly on monetization, so this chapter will consider the best ways to produce content that can generate sales.

As we have seen in previous chapters, we have to make a choice and set a goal. Basically, we have to understand that the way of communicating (and therefore of writing) has changed because people have changed their way of getting information and buying. We have to adapt to this change or we will be left behind. Customers don't want to know the description of the product or service but they want to know if and how it helps them solve a problem or offer them a change of perspective. And possibly, they want to know this as soon as possible.

How to create viral written content

There are the suggestions, the advice, the general indications and then there are the rules. In the next few pages you are going to learn the rules to create viral written content that sells like crazy. You have to always keep in mind the following 10 points.

- **The sentimental elements**. People love to remember the good old days, we are all a little nostalgic after all. Combine something from the past with your brand and insert these "nuggets of memories" into your content, able to transport the reader back in time. To achieve this, make use of "sensory" words, which arouse emotions in the reader.

- **The narcissistic elements.** Who is the person we love most in the world? Ourselves! We like it when those we know very little remember our name, we love to hear it pronounced, we spend hours in the mirror looking at ourselves. If you want to grab the attention of your readers, then you need to talk about them. Offer a stimulus to make them become protagonists, use everything you can to personalize the content to be sent to them, marking the title of an email with their first name, for example.

- **The competition.** Traditional marketing vs inbound marketing, Facebook vs LinkedIn, eBook vs paper book and on and on. Splitting your audience and encouraging people to take sides on one side or the other of a topic of interest to them is effective for creating viral content. Your content will be highly engaging and you will immediately be able to raise the level of brand awareness.

- **The irony**. An ironic touch must never be missing within the content you produce for your company.

Not taking yourself too seriously does not diminish the value of your brand or your skills in the industry. Being ironic is a talent, an extra gift, not something that harms your brand. Do not forget it as it could be of great importance.

- **Storytelling.** It is fundamental to be clear here, because a lot of social media marketers do not understand it. Storytelling does not mean telling a story. Not only that, at least. It is rather connected with engagement and brand awareness. The ability to excite, to make people think, to push people to rethink what they have read. A mix of memories, past, nostalgia but also experience to be shared to show by example how to face a difficulty and improve one's personal or professional condition in the future. Storytelling is such an amazing tool at your disposal, use it properly.

- **Personal hypothesis.** Not in all the contents we can insert a personal hypothesis on the subject but when this is possible, the engagement of people increases, because they are curious. In some types of text you can discuss a "thesis" or even present an "antithesis" which could be provocative. Do not be afraid to take a position.

- **The gratuity.** It is part of these 10 rules for creating winning content on the internet. Content, in addition to being useful, relevant and shared, must be free. The question at this point is the following one. Why do you have to offer your competence, your knowledge, your way of working for free to complete strangers? Because thanks to content marketing and the inbound approach, you will learn how to turn those strangers into paying customers for your company. Finding out "in theory" how a certain activity is done does not mean having the experience to put it into practice nor the time, budget or talent necessary, so the competition will always be ten steps behind if you start giving away free information. Furthermore, in this way you are able to build a good and healthy relationship with your followers and they will be ready to give you their money once you start selling.

- **Statistics**. People are always very attracted to statistics and data concerning other realities similar to theirs. The social proof note increases engagement. An example? 50% of the companies that decided to invest in a corporate blog immediately acquired new customers, compared to those that remained offline. Isn't that a fact that makes you think?

- **Active listening.** The best ideas for creating viral content for the web come from the readers themselves. Comments, reviews, messages left in Chat: listening means intercepting complaints, shortcomings, meeting new needs, seizing opportunities and finding successful trends to propose to your target audience.

- **Roll up your sleeves**. There are no shortcuts in content marketing. The results are guaranteed and measurable but it takes time, perseverance in carrying out the work, continuous updating and a lot of quality content. With this in mind, a long and comprehensive article published a couple of times a week on the corporate blog is preferable to an avalanche of short texts disconnected from your core business and used only as fillers for the pages of your blog.

For each type of content you propose, always ask yourself the following question. Am I really offering value to interested people who will read this post? If the answer is positive, then you are doing a great job. On the other hand, if you cannot say so, we encourage you to reconsider your strategy before doing more harm than good.

The rules for creating valuable online content

If the previous 10 rules are the orientation map, the following are the steps to take to reach the goal of creating engaging and powerful content online. In fact, in order to publish content on the web that gets more and more visibility over time, you must also think about pleasing Google's search engine. Here are a few tips on how to do it.

- **Write in a simple yet effective way**. Do not be trivial but simple and direct. If the reader has to go back and reread the sentence to understand it, you have lost his attention and Google will take notice of that.

- **Format the text to facilitate reading and allow the reader to "scan" the text quickly.** You can do this making use of bolds and paragraphs.

- **Use catchy headlines to grab attention and encourage people to read what you've written.** This is why the first few words of every article or post are very important for the success of the entire piece of content. Take the time to elaborate an impactful title before pressing the "publish" button.

- **Make use of bulleted lists (like this one) to help your audience understand the concepts.** Bulleted lists are a great way to split and explain content in an effective way. Make sure they are nicely formatted and you are ready to go.

- **Insert links within the text or image to other articles on your blog and to third party sites recognized as authoritative sources**. This practice is called cross-linking and it is extremely important to improve the reach of your content.

- **Choose your images carefully.** Photos and illustrations are not just white space fillers. The message must be complementary to that of the text, strengthening it but also communicating independently and enticing the reader. For example, you can do this by projecting in his mind what result he will achieve thanks to the solution you are proposing.

- **Learn to choose keywords carefully.** These are the keywords of your business, those that allow people to find you on Google and on the web. Their choice is strategic. In fact, a main keyword is enough for each text to be included in the introduction, then repeating it discursively in the body and in the conclusion. Take the time to study this topic very carefully as the success of your content depends on the keywords you decide to target.

- **Conclude with the Call-to-Action.** When you write content like this, you should always imagine that in the end the reader asks you what he should do. This is the perfect time to give him an answer using a call to action. This could be clicking a button, writing a comment or buying a product. The important thing is to never let your audience escape without having done something for you. After all, once you provide potential customers with free valuable content it is your right to ask for something in return.

Now that we have discussed the power of written content, it is time to dive deeper into the second most used form of content. We are talking about pictures and images.

Features of a great image

What are the characteristics that an image on Instagram must have to receive more engagement and increase followers? Are there any characteristics that all the images that get more likes have in common?

To give a precise answer to these questions, we carried out a survey on more than 8 million images published on Instagram based on about 30 visual parameters that connote a photo, in order to understand which features bring the most likes. Everything we discovered is summed up in seven. Here is what they are.

1. Brightness

The brightest photos win, because they convey greater positivity. Lighter images earn 24% more likes than similar images with darker tones. Obviously users are more inclined to give their appreciation to more heartening and reassuring visual content. Light colours certainly certainly communicate more pleasant and reassuring emotions than the same image with darker hues. After all, we are usually afraid of the dark, not of the light and what frightens or disturbs us hardly gains our approval.

Therefore, when you are creating an image for your business Instagram profile, make sure you are selecting light colours.

2. Background

A close-up on a background is preferred over an image that has no depth of field, in which the subject fills the whole picture. Art history scholars know this well, to the point that someone has even observed that the success in the collective imagination of a painting like Leonardo Da Vinci's La Gioconda does not derive only from the enigmatic nature of Mona Lisa's smile and gaze, but from the contrast between the perfect definition of the portrait of the woman and the vastness of the background behind it. In general, if you post a photo on Instagram with a large background and a nice depth behind it, you get 29% more likes than a flat photo without a background.

3. Dominant color

Blue-tinged images get 24% more likes than red-tinged ones. This is a less predictable result, which contrasts with a previous study titled "Why We Filter Photos and How It Affects Engagement" conducted by a team of three Yahoo Labs and one Georgia Tech University researchers, who had instead found that warmer colors lead to more interactions. In reality, the Yahoo-Georgia Tech study, which examined user behavior on Flickr rather than Instagram, is not focused on likes which are the minimum and most instinctive interactions implemented by users, but on interactions at a higher level of awareness and energy, especially comments and shares. If we refer to likes, it is possible that a more bluish tone of a photo is more reassuring and induces greater empathy with the contents of the photo, generating a like, while brighter colors infuse users with more vivid emotions and therefore lead them to express your opinion with greater commitment, i.e. with comments.As you should be able to understand by now, not all social media platforms are created equal and what works well on one could not be the best choice in absolute terms. Always take into consideration where you are posting your pictures, not only who is going to see them.

4. Number of dominant colors

If we publish an image with a single dominant color (whatever it is), we can expect 17% more likes than we would get by posting a photo with many contrasting colors. From a psychological point of view, it can be explained as follows: many colors with different shades, if they act in a contrasting effect, produce a disorientation of the user in the emotional resonance with the image. Put simply: too many colors are confusing. And we do not like to be confused.

5. Saturation

Images that are too saturated, too full of colors, create a sense of alarm that results in slight repulsion towards the image itself. This results in less engagement and likes. On the other hand, if you publish photos with more subdued tones, you immediately have a sense of greater visual mastery and a better general perception of the image, with the effect of granting your consent more easily. In short: a slightly saturated photo takes 18% more likes.

6. Texture

Images that are too clean and smooth are less appreciated than those that are rougher and more grainy. Probably because the latter are perceptually more stimulating, offering the eye something to focus its attention on immediately. In practice, an image that is too homogeneous does not offer the eye enough material to consider, requiring more attention. And by now you will have understood that if you have to pay more attention it means that more energy is required and the rational part of thinking is activated. Since we want to make our followers feel emotions, activating their brains too much is not effective to reach our goals. We know this could sound a bit funny, but it is true.

Images with a more dynamic texture get 79% more likes.

7. Selfies

It seems that selfies in which no faces are captured get 0% more likes than those with faces! This is a funny way of saying that there is no difference between the face you make, so don't squeeze your mouth in the belief that you are more attractive or interesting. People are interested in the quality of the photo in general, the attitude you convey as a whole while a grimace, alone, only shows that you have little style and even less imagination in introducing yourself. Our advice here is pretty simple: avoid unnatural poses, they don't make you earn just one more like.

Also, if you run a company or personal brand, we highly suggest you limit the use of selfies as they are often seen as unprofessional and silly. Stick to what works and do not improvise too much when you are starting out.

To conclude this chapter, we would like to discuss how to actually start taking pictures that are engaging and help your brand become more established online. Here are a few tips you can follow to ensure you do things the right way.

Creating posts on Instagram with the right and most effective images is a problem that everyone, users and companies, must face immediately after signing up to the social network. The impact with other users and much more experienced brands and with a dizzying number of likes and followers can be scary at first, but a few simple tricks will be enough to kick off a respectable career as an "Instagrammer".

1. Choose your focus

Talking (and posting) without knowing exactly what we want to communicate is equivalent to not talking at all, or worse to being branded as careless and uninteresting. The first step, therefore, is to know what we want to communicate with our images, whether our goal is to reveal what lies behind our products or services or whether it is simply to increase the number of our followers.

2. Choose your subject and composition carefully

our message, but which reflects our mission as well. Being light-hearted and not very formal is fine, but only if it is in line with our target and always without exaggerating. The composition of the image must then be harmonious: to start remember to respect the symmetry to give a sense of order and cleanliness.

3. Prefer a white background

For your photos to be successful on Instagram, you don't have to become a pairing expert or know the Pantone color palette by heart. Just make sure you have a white background available and you are good to go. In this way you will give greater prominence to the object you want to capture and you will ensure a nice photographic studio effect.

4. Avoid an excessive use of the flash!

We might be led to believe that the flash is the solution to any exposure problem, but it is not. In fact, the image will immediately appear more static, the colors will be altered and the result will be anything but accurate. We try to prefer natural light and consider the idea of investing in special tools. Remember that being a beginner is not a fault, but it shouldn't be used as an excuse to sacrifice quality.

5. Take more than one photo

Do you remember when there were only film cameras and in the case of official photos or important memories, the photographer asked you to remain in a pose to take another one for safety? Well, even for our posts on Instagram, the principle must be the same. You should treat yourself to more than one shot, perhaps changing the angle or composition. In this way, you will have much more choices available when it will be time to post something.

6. Be careful to choose the right filter

The creation of effective photos on Instagram cannot ignore the knowledge and choice of the most suitable filter. There are prodigious ones, able to make even the most anonymous photos exceptional. However, this should not be an excuse to take superficial pictures. We advise you to choose a filter and stick with it for a while in order to create consistency along your profile.

7. Practice makes perfect

The secret to mastering any art and tool is to practice consistently. Your posts will not suddenly succeed, but if you continue to pay attention to every aspect and measure the results of each of our actions, the effectiveness not only of the single post but also of your account in general will certainly increase over time. And, beyond the marketing goals you set for yourselves, taking photos on Instagram will become really fun and remunerative.

With these seven tips we can consider our discussion about the main strategies to create amazing and viral content concluded. Now you have to start putting these ideas into practice and implementing them over time, as this is the only way to actually see positive results.

Chapter 6

The Ideal Length of Posts

This chapter is going to be a goldmine of information for those that want to take their social media marketing skills to the next level. In fact, in the next few pages we are presenting you the exact length your posts should have depending on the social media platform you decide to use. Knowing these data will give you an unfair advantage over your competitors. Let's get started!

What is the ideal length of the post texts that are published in the main social media platforms? It's a question any professional social media manager has asked themselves to get the best results every time they create new content.

It is possible to give a precise answer, but a premise must be made. How do you evaluate the quality of a post on social media?

In abstract terms, a content can be evaluated for its level of depth, for its originality, for the richness of topics, for the ability to excite users. But when we consider social media posts, the issue takes on a different meaning and the first feature to be instilled in a post is its ability to be noticed and to stand out on the huge amount of content published incessantly every single day.

Basically, an excellent post in terms of content that is not noticed by any user is as if it had never been published. For a content manager or a social media marketing manager, therefore, it represents an effort not rewarded by a result.

The most direct estimate of interest in a post is based on the direct engagement of the user, who, struck by the value of the post itself, implements a form of interaction, such as a like, a comment or a share.

It must be said that not all social media users are inclined to actively interact with posts. In fact, a reliable estimate indicates that no more than 25% of users actually engage in interactions. Furthermore, these interactions usually increase with the degree of relational closeness that one has with the user who published the post. In general, however, a post that receives many interactions in relation to the amount of views it has obtained through the social media algorithm is a successful post.

In summary, therefore, the most typical measure of the success of an online post is the amount of interactions it has received, which represents the engagement obtained. Of course, this value also depends on the amount of contacts of the user who publishes the post, so users with many followers and friends are much more likely to receive interactions. This is because the post will be viewed by a higher number of people and therefore the possibility of collecting an initial number of interactions is more consistent.

Furthermore, the level of active engagement collected by a post follows the preferential attachment rule. This is the phenomenon whereby a certain benefit is assigned more to those subjects to whom that same benefit has already been given. Put simply, the rich are getting richer, while the poor are getting poorer. This is also known as the Matthew effect. In this sense, posts that have already received many interactions are more likely to receive more likes than those posts that have received fewer engagement.

Those users who have a large amount of followers can therefore hope to quickly have a first critical mass of interactions that create a flywheel that progressively attracts more and more interactions.

On this basis, the initial question then becomes the following. How should you build a post in order to get the maximum number of interactions as soon as possible?

A determining factor (although obviously not the only one) is the length of the text of which the post is composed. Posts with very long descriptive texts usually get lower engagement than those with very direct and incisive texts. However, the optimal size varies from social media to social media, because each platform has specificities that affect the optimal length of the text. So let's see what is the ideal length of the texts to be published in each social media.

The ideal length of texts in Facebook

In organic posts the practice of maximum brevity applies. In 2020 BuzzSumo analyzed more than 800 million Facebook posts, noticing that posts with less than 50 characters have more engagement than posts with longer texts. Jeff Bullas has also done his own study on this and the result is that posts with no more than 80 characters receive a 66% higher engagement than all the others.

It is not difficult to explain why this happens. On the one hand, there are cognitive barriers: the longer a post is, the greater the mental effort required to obtain the overall meaning of the information and therefore the more difficult it is to achieve full satisfaction or involvement that leads to interaction. This is especially true in contexts defined by social media, in which the level of attention and brain activity given to each post tends to be very low. Another reason is of a technical nature. In fact, beyond a certain number of characters, the text is truncated and to read it the user needs to click on the post itself. Most users, if they do not immediately find the content of the visible part of the text interesting, do not click and therefore the probability of engagement is reduced to almost zero.

In the case of advertising, the situation becomes even more rigid. Each Facebook ad currently consists of three parts of text: the Main Text (the one at the top and represents the actual caption of the ad), the Title (the one found under the image or video and usually it is the one that most attracts attention) and the Description (which is found under the Title and which is not always present in the advertisements).

Just to give you an idea, an effective title must have no more than 5 words, the main text no more than 14 and the description no more than 18.

The ideal length of texts in Instagram

Instagram, much more than Facebook, is based on vi-sual content. The text is therefore read by people only after they have been conquered by the image.

This does not mean, however, that any text is created equal. In fact, the texts that most of all manage to engage users and lead them to engagement are those that do not exceed 125 characters.

Furthermore, if in general the use of hashtags in Facebook is completely pleonastic, in Instagram it is indispensable. But how many hashtags should be included in a text? Although you can enter up to 30, posts with 9 to 12 hashtags get more interactions.

The ideal length of texts in Twitter
In Twitter there is no room for long texts. The peremptory length of a tweet is currently 280 characters, but on average the most effective posts in generating interactions are those that do not exceed 100 characters.
As for hashtags, the winning posts are those that include no more than 3.

The ideal length of texts in LinkedIn

In LinkedIn, a distinction must be made between posts and articles.

The perfect posts to create engagement are those that have a text with no more than 140 characters. On LinkedIn, longer posts are truncated as well.

The most engaging articles have an ideal length between 1,900 and 2,000 words, corresponding to approximately 10,000 characters. Under this length, more or less everyone gets the same results, even in terms of average visibility.

The ideal length of texts in YouTube

YouTube compared to other social networks is much more based on searches made by users. In this sense, the use of the site is very similar to that of a real search engine having videos as its object. For this reason it is essential that the accompanying texts of the published videos have within them the keywords that best represent the content.

In terms of length, the title text should not exceed 70 characters, while the description text should be within 160 characters. Usually in YouTube there is very little use of hashtags, but there are more and more analysts who instead suggest inserting some well chosen hashtags in the description.

Now that you have discovered this powerful information, we need to talk about another important topic when it comes to content marketing. In fact, if now you know how to properly set up an editorial plan and how to create engaging articles and images, you still have to learn what the KPIs are. The next chapter is going to tell you everything about them.

Chapter 7

The Most Relevant KPIs to Consider

When implementing a content marketing strategy, it is also essential to define how to evaluate its success and effectiveness. The quality of the content production actions depends first of all on the reactions that the target audience expresses following the use of the content itself. These reactions can be of various kinds and it is up to the content marketer to detect them and measure their extent.

In fact, one of the typical errors of content marketing activities is the absence of a systematic control plan for the effects produced by the published content. Unlike other forms of marketing that are directly linked to a well-defined number of key performance indicators (KPIs) that easily define their success or failure, content marketing establishes a relationship with users in the longer term and less immediately linked to conversions or specific measurable actions.

In other words, the content is often seen as a value in itself, a point of contact with the potential or current customer that simply serves to reaffirm the value of the company, its prestige and the quality of the products It is very rare to have a precise view of the content as a stage in the customer journey that leads the customer to the purchase.

To evaluate the value of a content - and therefore more generally of the content marketing strategy implemented - it is necessary to see the content itself as the origin of a series of behaviors induced in a predetermined way that affect its user. Thanks to the content, the user is encouraged to carry out specific actions that push him forward on the path that will eventually lead him to conclude a purchase.

It is these specific actions that the content can generate that infuse value into the content itself. To understand if a content marketing strategy works and is success-oriented, we must ask ourselves what the actions that the published contents induce to take are and how to measure them.

At the end of 2020 Hubspot published a survey carried out on approximately 3,400 marketing managers around the world to derive the trends and prevailing opinions of experts on a variety of topics. The question "How do you measure the success of your content marketing strategy?" produced the following responses.

- Increased authority;
- Success in SEO;
- Traffic on the website;
- Engagement on the site;
- Social engagement;
- Lead generation;
- Total sales generated;

Let's look at each of these aspects to better understand how it can help gauge the value of a content marketing strategy. As always we will keep an eye on our end goal: monetization.

Increased authority

As we said, the first aspect - and often the only one - that is attributed to good content is the feeling it transmits to the user. Basically, good content amplifies the perception of the brand and the perceived value of the products and services.
In general, good content increases brand awareness. This is also true in terms of personal branding, when the content serves to give prestige to the author who produced it.

The publication of valuable content allows the company to achieve a higher E-A-T value. This means it increases the public's attribution (T) of a high level of expertise, an immediately perceptible authorship (A) and a consolidated trustworthiness (T). It should also be emphasized that a high E-A-T value helps a company and its site to be recognized by Google as deserving of a high ranking, so the production of valuable content contributes to improving the SEO positioning of the entire site.

If on the one hand the increase in brand awareness and E-A-T are the main reasons that convince companies to adopt content marketing strategies, on the other hand these aspects are the most difficult to measure in the real results achieved. For this purpose, useful quantitative KPIs can be the time spent on the page, as well as the collection of analytical data that allow us to understand the way in which the user has visited the content page (detecting scrolls, clicks and mouse movements) highlighting which are the areas on which he focused most.

However, these are parameters that do not give a precise idea of the interest shown, nor of the sentiment that the user has made of the topics covered. In order to obtain more precise qualitative information, surveys should be carried out, in order to identify the impressions and points of view of users at the end of the use of a content or a series of contents.

In some cases it might be useful to insert a short survey right at the end of an article. You can also ask a single closed question, which a percentage of users could answer. The percentage of responses to the survey, compared to the total number of users who visited the content page, is in itself an indicator of the level of interest and engagement aroused by the content. Reading and classifying the responses received, it is possible to obtain valuable information on the sentiment referred to the specific content, the brand and the products.

Other surveys can be done through pop-ups on the company website, as well as through specific campaigns in social networks.

An effective technique for obtaining information on sentiment using social networks can be implemented by following the following steps.

- Publish one or more important content on the company blog.

- Sponsor these contents on Facebook on a well-defined target audience.

- Create a custom audience made up of all the people who have visited the content pages and this audience is targeted by a survey via a new campaign.

- Create a control group by simultaneously addressing the survey to a target audience with the same characteristics from which, however, users who have visited the site are excluded.

The comparison between the answers given by people who have used the content and those who have not used it allows you to understand what the effect generated by the content itself may be.

Success in SEO

Another aspect that marketers take into strong consideration is the acquisition of relevant positions in search engines thanks to the published content. Many companies are inclined to invest in a blog to improve SEO, using posts to link the brand and products to a number of relevant keywords that could not be included directly on the corporate website.

Doing a search and finding the content in the top positions of the SERP always gives reasons for satisfaction and many content managers are already fully satisfied when this happens. In reality, two main factors must be taken into consideration before claiming victory.

1. Are the keywords corresponding to the positioning of the content really relevant for your company? There is little point in placing content at the top of the search for "the best Dalmatian dog food" if the company sells products for cats.

2. What traffic is actually generated by the ranking obtained? Writing a 15,000-character article to rank first on an absolutely niche search query that users never search for means no real advantage.

The KPIs that measure SEO success are obviously those that relate to positioning on a more or less broad set of keywords of interest. But obviously those that define the volumes of organic traffic generated by a certain positioning must also be considered.

In particular, it is appropriate to note both the direct traffic that is induced on the content itself by its positioning in the search engines, and the indirect traffic that, starting from the organic traffic generated, leads to any call to action present in the content. Through appropriate analysis systems like Google Analytics it is possible to identify the volume of traffic generated from simple searches that arrives on the landing page of the call to action. In this way it is possible to evaluate the effective traffic obtained by the positioning in the results page.

Traffic on the company or personal brand website

Site traffic is another success factor that is considered by most content managers. It consists of the number of users who have visited the content or other pages of the site starting from the call to action or simply from the links included in the content.

It is therefore necessary to distinguish the traffic absorbed by the page where the content is located from the traffic generated by the content to other pages of the site.

In the first case, the page on which the volume of traffic produced by the content develops can be on the company website, but it can also be an external page, for example in a third-party blog or on a social network. The main KPI in this case is the amount of users who have seen the content.

In this way, the impact of the content on the public is measured and therefore the level of interest that the content has aroused can be discovered. In fact, to get a more precise idea, you should also add the time spent on the page. If the time is very low, it is clear that most users do not find the content interesting.

But be careful when doing this. In fact, traffic is not a significant index of the intrinsic value of a content. A mediocre content pushed through advertising campaigns will register much more traffic than a valid one entrusted only to organic visits. Furthermore, even just by comparing the organic traffic, if a content has been lucky enough to position itself better on search engines and in relation to keywords that are highly researched by users, it will get much more traffic than another content that it has not positioned itself well.

Furthermore, certain lighter and more trivial content can be much more stimulating for users thus generating more traffic, but from the point of view of quality, this type of content will not give particular benefits to the company or personal brand in terms of awareness and engagement.

Traffic on content is therefore a simple indicator of the visibility of the content itself, not of its success for marketing purposes.

In this sense, it is more interesting to measure the amount of traffic generated on the company's website or other significant pages from the content. In the content or on the page where it is located, there may be links or calls to action that lead to other pages where, for example, the user can perform specific actions, such as subscribing to a newsletter, downloading an ebook, buying a product or scheduling a call.

In this case, the interesting KPI is the bounce rate, which is the percentage of users who enter and leave the page where the content is located without having performed the call to action. The percentage of users leaving the site from that specific content is also relevant. In fact, it indicates how many users did not consider it interesting to continue visiting the site after having seen that content.

If, on the other hand, the content is on an external website, it is important to note how much traffic arrives at the company site or on landing pages created ad hoc starting from the links included in the content itself. It is possible to collect this data using Google Analytics, setting the site where the content is located as the traffic source and the company site as the point of arrival. It is thus possible to understand if the content published is effective in bringing users to areas of the site that can lead to conversions or if it is useless in doing that.

Engagement on the site

When in the first decade of the 2000s blogs began to become one of the most popular online communication tools, their primary feature was the opportunity given to users to leave comments directly on the same page where the content was published. Today interactions of this kind are less and less numerous, because users prefer to comment on social networks rather than blogs.

Today blogs have lost a large part of their primary function, that is to create a space for dialogue with the public directly on the site where the original content is published. But on the other hand, the areas of interaction in the sites have become much more numerous than those that were available in the first years of the new millennium and support customer engagement in an increasingly broad and satisfying way.

Reviews, ratings and chat in real time allow users to have their say and to converse directly with the managers of a website.

The success of a content can also be seen in the ability to stimulate users to get in touch with authors and company managers in charge of relations with the public. Measuring the engagement induced by one or more contents therefore becomes a way to understand if you are doing a good job or not. Content that arouses interactions on the site creates a high level of user engagement and therefore an increase in the value attributed to the brand, products and in general the company's communication style.

A user who is very involved in a relationship with company staff or who feels the need to express himself directly to the company is a potential customer who is increasingly moving towards the phases of the customer journey closest to the purchase decision.

The KPIs useful for measuring engagement are obviously those that count the overall amount of interactions generated by a single piece of content. While it is easy to enumerate comments or ratings comparing them to the total number of visits received by a blog post, in many cases it is more complicated to understand if a certain content has generated the sending of a message to a company manager via the chat integrated into the site.

Also in this case it is possible to have this type of information simply by asking the user who opens the chat conversation what convinced him to get in touch with the company staff. In this way it is possible to directly understand which contents have aroused interest and therefore if the marketing activities oriented to the relationship with current and potential customers are having success.

In some ways, the interaction with banners and advertising of various kinds inserted on the page can also be considered as engagement. In this case, the results of interaction with these advertisements can be related to the number of views of the content in order to have an estimated percentage of the capability to enhance the advertising conveyed by the content.

In this way, an economic value can be given to the content itself in terms of the value generated by the interaction with advertising. From the point of view of content marketing, the publisher who publishes the content receives an income based on the number of click-throughs generated on an ad, so it is possible to economically enhance a content based on the advertising revenue generated.

Social engagement

As we said, most of the conversations and the most advanced forms of engagement have now moved to social networks. Sharing content on a page, in groups or in some profile can generate many interactions. The best way, however, is to sponsor the content and make it visible to the highest degree to a well-defined target audience. Facebook allows you to create campaigns aimed at collecting interactions, maximizing the social engagement effects that good content can produce.

In this context, if the content is well constructed and accompanied by the right introductory text, it can become a real magnet for likes and comments.

The KPIs to keep under control in social networks tend to be the most typical of social media marketing, in particular the engagement rate and the click-through rate (CTR), as well as obviously the amount of views the content gets.

Lead generation

One of the most important content purposes is lead generation. Quality content may contain a call to action that entices a user to subscribe to a newsletter by leaving their contact details (usually their email or phone number).

However, you can also equip the published content with additional in-depth content that can only be seen after leaving the contact details. The result is the acquisition of a large number of leads, which can then be reused for email marketing or other forms of direct contact, with implementation logics consistent with those of all other digital marketing activities.

The most significant KPIs are precisely those related to the measurement of the lead generation rate in relation to visits to the content page. They are very significant KPIs, because they can directly and punctually evaluate the level of interest actually produced by a single piece of content.

Only the most effective and valuable content can convert users into leads.

A lead is obviously of great value for a company, because it represents a highly motivated potential customer which should be easily convertible to a paying client. Therefore, content that produces a lot of leads is content that demonstrates that the content marketing strategy put in place is doing very well.

Total sales

Content that can directly entice a user to make a purchase is the ideal content to have on your website or social media profile. Together with lead generation, the total sales number is the parameter that allows to attribute a direct economic value to the content you publish.

Many contents simply contain more or less contextualized links or banners that lead to pages where you can buy a product.

Other contents are built specifically to entice users to make an immediate purchase.

Content of this type, when it is effective and aimed at a target audience can lead to a conversion.

The KPI to consider in this case is precisely the ratio between completed conversions (purchases) and the number of visitors to the site.

It is clear that the implementation of an effective content marketing strategy must be completed by the identification of a series of KPIs useful for identifying the value and success of the actions carried out. In this way the company can truly insert content marketing among the formulas that in the medium-long term can bring significant results and integrate it into a broad-spectrum digital marketing strategic plan, which includes both inbound marketing actions and direct contact with the public.

As you might have noticed, there is not a single KPI that can tell you if your content marketing strategy is doing well or not. Each piece of content you publish has its own goal and its effectiveness should be measured accordingly.

By now you should have a very clear idea of what content marketing is and how an editorial plan can be put in place and evaluated over time. Now it is time to focus on the different social media platforms to use to maximize the reach of your content.

Before moving on, we warmly advise you to read these last four chapters again as they are the base for what is coming in the next pagest. Also, we feel it would be valuable for you to follow along and craft your editorial plan before reading the next chapter.

Chapter 8

Facebook for Your Business or Personal Brand

With this chapter we begin our discussion of the main social media marketing platforms available to businesses and personal brands. We feel we could not start talking about the various social media without starting from the first real social network used for marketing purposes. We are clearly talking about Facebook and the next few chapters will tell you everything you need to know about it.

In fact, small and medium-sized businesses can implement Facebook marketing strategies with high margins of success. With more than 2 billion active users every month, it is not possible to exclude the blue social network from your web marketing plan.

What can be the goals of Facebook marketing for businesses and personal brands? Let's take a look at them.

Brand awareness

Facebook is a very important tool to allow small and medium-sized enterprises to make their products and services known online, while cultivating a very direct relationship with interested users.

If on the one hand your community, made up of people who already know the company's products, can follow it on the blue social network, on the other hand it is also possible to reach people who do not know it through spontaneous sharing or through sponsored ads. The latter, through the creation of the right audience, allow you to reach new people potentially interested in the products or services that your company offers on the market.

Customer care

Facebook is also one of the places on the web that is best suited for customer care.

Promotional content can still be valid, but using your social page as a place to solve the problems and perplexities of your users can be a highly useful way to use Facebook, precisely because it is capable of triggering conversations between friends, debates and engagement which is greatly appreciated by Facebook's algorithms.

Direct sales

Facebook can also be used to sell your own products or services. If the company has an e-commerce site, Facebook allows you to increase the chances of success in online sales. For example, you can create a product catalog and then insert them on your business page, as well as create particular types of ads (called offers) precisely to entice the user to make a purchase without further thinking.

Obviously it must be said that those who have an important business in their hands cannot simply rely on

Zuckerberg's social network to market their products online, but it is a fact that not a month goes by in which the Menlo Park team does not make available some new function that favors those who want to sell using Facebook.

Lead generation

Collecting as many contact details of current and potential customers is vital for small businesses and personal brands. Through emails, phone numbers or other forms of direct contact, companies can address increasingly personal and targeted messages to their audience, especially if they know how to use marketing automation techniques.

Facebook allows you to collect this type of data, making it possible for the company to combine the sending of private messages with broader forms of communication. Among the forms of advertising that Facebook offers to companies is the collection of leads. Basically, an user who sees the ad and is attracted to it can be persuaded to provide your company with their contact details while remaining within Facebook. In this way, the number of contacts that your company manages to acquire is higher than that procured by other forms of lead generation.

Creating a successful Facebook marketing strategy

Before actually starting to take action on Facebook, it is good for small and medium-sized businesses to take the time to create a well-researched and designed communication plan.

First of all, the goals of the strategies to be implemented on the blue social network must be defined.

Secondly, the target audience must be identified, tracing a sort of identity of its main characteristics such as age, place of residence, interests, level of education and income.

As for the contents, it will be good to dedicate only 20% of posts to the promotion of products or services so as not to tire the users with continuous offers and hype.

Finally, the tools for controlling results should not be forgotten. For example, if the goal is to set up helpful customer care systems, one of the ways to evaluate the effectiveness of the actions carried out is to analyze the number and quality of comments received, rather than that of 'likes'.

Facebook advertising

If in the past Facebook was the realm of free communication, based on direct relationship actions and visibility linked to the quality of the posts published, today this is no longer the case. The new algorithms tend to heavily reduce the organic visibility of contents, especially when they are published in company pages. The only way to guarantee valuable results is by planning paid advertising campaigns, which can allow you to reach the most targeted audience for the company in a precise and effective way.

Small businesses and personal brands can find in Facebook the most suitable channel for their communication, because at a small cost great results can be achieved. The problem is that most small and medium-sized businesses don't have people who know Facebook and its marketing communication tools in-house. The consequence is that many companies give up using Facebook or rely on operators of dubious competence, who are not able to bring real benefits to the company business or personal brand.

To solve this problem, we have decided to dedicate the next few pages to understand how to properly use Facebook in an effective way.

Chapter 9

The Perfect Facebook Post

Before looking at how to use Facebook ads to gather new leads and sales, it is important to discuss how to write an effective Facebook post.

Writing successful text posts on Facebook is getting harder and harder. In fact, since 2013 the organic reach has decreased dramatically. You can't get the same number of views that you once got without paying.

Today Facebook requires the payment of a donation to obtain noteworthy results. Paid ads have become a must to become visible to your target audience.

Moreover, Facebook can afford to ask for payments in this regard. It's about business. There are 2 billion monthly active users, while the pages of small businesses amount to about 60 million: to emerge from this ocean and get noticed you have to pay via Facebook Ads. But in cases where you are on a tight budget, how can you increase the organic reach of Facebook post views? What are the strategies for creating effective and engaging text posts?

In an era where visual posts based on images and videos reign supreme, textual content can still be effective. Social media marketing still needs words to communicate to its audience. But to write successful text posts on Facebook you need to follow certain criteria.

Length of the text

By scrolling through Facebook's News Feed during their daily scroll, users have no intention of getting involved in long texts. The writing of excessively long posts should therefore be avoided. However, it is true that by scrolling through the post, many will read the first few lines, which are decisive for engagement purposes. A textual post that presents interesting starting phrases can convince the reader to continue reading even a text that is not exactly short.

To attract attention, a captivating question can be asked, a fact of emotional impact can be immediately revealed, an intuition can be referred to, phrases and expressions capable of attracting attention can be used.

Style and content of the post

As for the style it is good to use an extremely simple one. Sentences that are too long and complex which can tire the reader should be avoided. It is necessary to resort to simple and short sentences with a vocabulary that is neither technical nor excessively refined.

As for the contents, it must be remembered that storytelling can be very successful precisely because it manages to touch the emotional levers of users, as we have mentioned in a previous chapter as well. You must not be afraid to also tell the difficulties, challenges and hard moments that your brand has had to go through, just to conclude with a note of positivity and hope. In fact, this type of storytelling manages to create empathy, sympathy and real engagement.

Structure of written posts

It is also very important to take into account the structure of a written post. The so-called structure of the inverted pyramid should be considered. In fact, the conclusions and key points of the speech will be written in the first part of the text. In this way, users will know from the start what they will get if they continue reading the post. In the body of the text, the details and all other further information can then be included.

Links

Facebook's algorithms are assumed to penalize posts with links by further reducing the organic reach. Many marketers to remedy the problem include the link in the comments. However, this way of operating means that users will have to take an extra action, not only having to read the post but also check the comments to look for the link. It is clear that this clumsiness can limit clicks on the link. So what to do?

A tip is to insert links directly in the text of the post, limiting yourself to doing so only in cases of real need.

Chapter 10

A Basic Introduction to Facebook Ads

With this chapter we begin our discussion about Facebook ads. They are an incredible tool at your disposal to increase your leads and to get more sales. They are extremely complex, so follow along to get a complete understanding of how they work.

A generic advertising campaign on Facebook has a structure consisting of three hierarchically decreasing levels. It is a sort of step pyramid model, where at the highest point is the first level called Campaign, further down we find the second level which is called Ad Groups. Finally, in the lowest and widest part of the pyramid there is the Ads section. Since the Campaign section is at the top of the pyramid, this will be unique. Within the same Facebook advertising campaign, we can find multiple ad groups. Finally, there can be multiple ads in a single ad group.

It is a structure that has a precise internal hierarchy, as mentioned, decreasing from top to bottom. In this sense, if you delete a campaign, all the ad groups and all the ads that were present in it will be deleted. If you delete a given group of listings, all listings in it will be removed as well. While if you delete a single advertisement, the others will not be deleted.

The levels of the Facebook Ads structure

The tiered structure of advertising campaigns on Facebook Ads is not an end in itself, but it makes sense to allow the construction of a campaign step by step, section by section.

Campaign

It is the first level of the Facebook Ads structure. It is the most important hierarchically. Inside there is the goals section. In fact, the goal must be set at the campaign level. There are three macro categories which are the following.

- Notoriety (with the goals: Brand awareness and Coverage);

- Engagement (with the goals Traffic, Interaction, App installation, Video views, Generation of contacts, Messages)

- Conversion (with the goals Conversions, Sale of catalog products, Visits to the store)

Only one goal can be defined for each campaign.

Ad Groups

It is the second level of the Facebook ads structure. The specifications relating to Audience, Positioning, Budget and scheduling must be set within it. Each group will have its own budget, positioning and audience. The presence of multiple ad groups for the same campaign allows for example to change a single parameter, leaving the others identical among the remaining ad groups. In this way it is possible to test the same ad on different audiences or with different placements in the various areas where Facebook allows you to view the ads.

Ads section

The ad is the last level of the Facebook ads hierarchy. In this section you can define the parameters relating to Format, Multimedia content and Additional Creativity. So at this level you will be able to decide what type of advertisement to insert: a single image, a carousel or a video. In addition to that you will also have to insert the right Call to action and the link. Multiple ads can be created for the same ad group, for example with different creatives. In this way, by analyzing the performance of individual ads you will be able to understand which advertising has had the most effective impact on the audience.

Advertising on Facebook is currently one of the forms of advertising with the best cost to benefit ratio. Although the cost of ads is slowly and steadily increasing, publishing a paid ad on Zuckerberg's platform means reaching your paying clients and potential customers in an extremely targeted way and therefore paying exclusively to reach the recipients of a perfectly targeted campaign. For this reason, in any planning of a social media marketing strategy, Facebook must always be present.

Let's take a look at some key points to keep in mind when creating your first Facebook ad.

We should start by saying that giving advice on how to create a successful advertising campaign in Facebook Ads is not easy. Anyone who has tried promoting a post on social media knows how often it happens not to reach the expected goals, failing to get even a good number of views.

Positive results are obtained in a Facebook advertising campaign not only when you are able to show the ad to a large number of users, but also when you are able to intercept the people in target, those who are most likely interested in the ad that you are promoting. It would actually make no sense to show an advertisement to a thousand people of whom only ten would be interested. It would be a waste of time and resources.

So how do you optimize the results? How to create a successful Facebook Ads? Here are 3 useful tips.

Consider the entire sales funnel

The ultimate goal of all social media marketing operations is being able to get users to buy your products or services. Considering the sales funnel, which is the journey that a generic consumer makes through different stages of interest before getting to buy, the conversion is the last act of a work made up of several parts. Instead, every step in the prospect's journey must be taken into consideration.

In fact, not all users are ready to buy. Some potential customers may not know you yet, they may have many doubts. Don't just focus on hot prospects, those ready to make a purchase. It would be a serious mistake. We need to feed all users, at whatever stage of the funnel they are.

Thus the ads on Facebook must aim not only to obtain the conversion, but also to increase the brand awareness of the company and to stimulate the needs of users in order to generate the desire to buy.

In this sense, it is not only necessary to launch campaigns aimed at selling, in which a product is presented and immediate purchase is proposed. It is very useful to advertise even broader contents, which perhaps speak of the methods of use of a possible product, of the contexts of use, of the cases in which the product can be useful, of experiences of use of the product by other users, etc.

In other cases, you can run a campaign that aims to engage users, asking them questions or proposing to carry out specific actions, such as posting photos, going to a store to get a reward and anything else you might be thinking about. On the other hand, when aiming at direct sales, communication must be optimized, with formulas that incentivize the purchase decision.

Use emojis

It has been observed that posts that featured emojis get more consideration than those without them. Smilies can make the announcement more fun, humane and light. This should result in greater engagement. However, this is a field very far from scientific logic. So, in this regard, all you have to do is test which emoji has the greatest impact on your target audience.

In general, you should always try to make posts as emotional as possible. It is also good practice to customize the message on the user's possible needs or experiences, in order to engage with him at the maximum degree.

Produce neutral launches

Neutrality is alien to the logic of marketing. You always tend to surround your brand with enthusiastic words, all devoted to positivity. Yet it has been shown that a neutral ad is very welcome and considered by users of the social network. Why is that the case? Because people generally want to be able to form their opinion on their own. They don't want cues, they don't want guides for their thoughts. In essence, engaging is fine, but trying to force the user to do something should be avoided. Otherwise, the risk is to annoy potential customers with the effect of leading them to raise defensive barriers against the company and its products. And in this case, you could say goodbye to conversions.

Chapter 11

Creating Your First Ad

Facebook Ads is the tool created by Facebook to create and manage advertising campaigns. These can be conveyed on Facebook and Instagram, but also on other websites that rent advertising space to Facebook.

Almost all of Facebook's revenue depends on ads, which have now become a favorite tool for marketers around the world.

By using Facebook Ads well, you can ensure your business has a stable source of new leads and customers. Compared to traditional advertisements, such as television and radio, Facebook offers you the possibility to choose with great care the people to whom you want to show your advertisements;

moreover, it is easy to monitor results and return on investment.

The potential is enormous, but there are also several technicalities and strategies to be known. In this chapter we will open the gates of this know-how, accrued with hundreds of thousands of dollars invested in Facebook Advertising on our behalf.

Before advertising on Facebook, you should make sure you have the following things set in place.

- **A business page on Facebook, and maybe a business Instagram profile.** Both of them should have all of your contact information, a good level of updating and curated images.

- A fast and functional website, which will help you host the "landing page" (we'll get to it in a moment) and present your company in a winning way.

- **A fairly precise idea of your customers' purchasing process.** Do they prefer to talk to a salesperson or go to the purchase immediately? What information do they need to convince themselves to buy? What are the main sources of distrust that can block them from expressing interest?

Once these three points are no longer a problem, it's time to start advertising on Facebook.

The reason why you shouldn't miss this tool is very simple: it is one of the most effective ways to make your company known; but above all, it is one of the best ways to have a positive return on advertising.

The return on advertising spend (ROAS) is the ratio between the money invested in advertising and the revenues you got.

In the future, things may take a different turn, but in the medium term, advertising campaigns on Facebook and Instagram will remain an exceptional tool from a ROAS point of view.

How to create a new campaign and how Facebook Ads campaigns are structured

If you want to have full control of your Facebook advertising, the first thing to do is to open a Business Manager.

Commonly called "BM", it is a profile from which you can manage all your activities and related advertising campaigns. To open one, simply go to www.business.facebook.com, register and link the account to your profile.

Once your Business Manager is ready, you can create a BM for each business whose Facebook page you manage.

Warning. to be able to do all this procedure by yourself, you must be the administrator of your company page. Any other role requires the authorization of an admin.

Once you have set this up you will be ready to start creating your first campaign.

The goals of a campaign

Speaking between entrepreneurs, the ultimate goal of an advertising campaign is to increase the company's profit. But we regret to tell you that Facebook Ads does not have a "Make money" button. In fact, it is up to you to figure out how to get there.

The goals we can pursue are different. When we create a campaign, Facebook will ask us to choose between the following.

- **Awareness**. This is the goal of a campaign aimed at showing the company to people, simply with the aim of making us known. It is divided into the following categories.
    - Brand awareness
    - Local awareness
    - Reach

- **Consideration**. This is the goal of a campaign that aims to make people interact with our company. The sub-goals are the following.
    - Traffic
    - Engagement

- App installation
- Video views
- Lead generation

- **Conversion**. These are campaigns that have the explicit goal of selling to the customer immediately after he has viewed the advertisement. The sub-goals are the following.
  - Sales
  - Catalog sales
  - Shop visits

The real goals of Facebook campaigns

As we have just seen, you have 14 goals to choose the ideal one for your campaign. There are several.

Are you confused? Don't worry, we'll make it easy for you to choose. Of these 14 goals, 11 are almost unused (or more frankly useless). The 3 really effective are the following.

- **Brand awareness.** It seems made to make small businesses known, but works well in reverse. It is especially useful for already large companies, which want to remind their customers of their existence.

- **Lead generation.** This is a very powerful tool, ideal for attracting the interest of potential customers and then cultivating it via email or telephone.

- **Sales**. It works well for companies that sell products costing less than $50, because it allows you to attract people's interest and then immediately conclude an impulsive sale.

However, we have to say that many companies continue to waste money on campaigns with exotic or wrong goals, so keep these valuable insights into consideration when you create your first ad.

Targeting section - audience choice

Let's forget about that story that a good salesman can sell ice to the Eskimos. A good salesman, if he goes to the North Pole, it does it to sell stoves.

On Facebook it works exactly the same way. In front of different people, you sell different products. And thanks to the significant amount of information Facebook collects about its users, we can be very specific in defining our audience.

Do you want to reach single women with two cats? No problem. Married couples with children aged 3 to 6 planning a vacation? You only need to ask. Off-site students with a passion for fitness? You will be satisfied.

Mainly there are three types of audiences you can reach on Facebook, explained individually in the next three paragraphs.

1. Custom audience

The first thing you can do is manually choose the characteristics of your audience. Here you can indulge yourself, choosing freely between the following data fields.

- Age

- Sex
- Interests
- Working condition
- Political and religious orientation
- Family situation
- Shopping habits
- Geographic location

And these are just some of the various parameters you can use to meticulously refine the audience to target your ads.

Furthermore, for each advertising campaign, you can choose to create ad sets that appeal to different audiences; we will see it better in the section dedicated to A/B testing.

Either way, your first ad campaign is very likely to use a custom audience as the target.

2. Retargeting

You launched your first campaign aimed at a custom audience, but you noticed a curious thing. Many people add products to their cart and then don't complete the purchase, or they leave their email but don't read your newsletter.

Something needs to be done to target those people again. They are so close to becoming your customers, yet so far away if you do not do the right thing.

Luckily you can reach them with a retargeting audience. "Re-targeting" means showing advertisements to an audience made up of people who have already interacted with you in the past.

You can choose to retarget people who have done one or more of the following things.

- Interacted with your page;
- Visited your site;
- Demonstrated interest in your posts;
- Seen your videos on Facebook;
- Left their contact details in the form of your lead generation campaign;
- Visited a specific page on your site.

In this way you can give them an extra push, and convince them to buy.

If you want to retarget people who have interacted with your Facebook page, you don't have to worry about a single thing. In fact, you just need to select the audience you are interested in and you are ready to launch the retargeting campaign.

If, on the other hand, you want to retarget who has visited your site, or a specific page, you will have to take care to install the Facebook Pixel. There is a lot to be said about the pixel, but here we need to reduce it to a minimum.

In short, the pixel is a piece of code that you can install on your site to allow Facebook to keep track of who visits it.
Facebook allows you to use the data collected by your pixel to create an audience to target ads. It is a pretty advanced feature, so do not worry about it when you are just starting out.

3. Lookalike Audience

Once you have launched your first campaigns, you start to have solid data. You have a nice list of email addresses of people who have bought from you, or a well-fed pixel of buyer data.

Now you can take this game to the next level.

Using a Lookalike Audience, you can create an audience of people similar to those who bought from you. Facebook will directly figure out who is similar to your customers, using its artificial intelligence.

You just have to choose how similar you want the people to be reached by the ads. You can choose a value from 1 (very similar) to 10 (vaguely similar).
A curious fact is that very often, the audiences with the closest resemblance to those who have already bought are not the ones that perform best.

The costs

This question is as frequent as it is wrong. If we put it under another perspective, you will see it immediately.

How much does it cost to play on the stock market?

First of all, costs must be distinguished from investments. Facebook campaigns are a means that, if managed well, serves to multiply the investment in advertising with a concrete economic return.

And this happens pretty fast too; in many cases, before the Facebook invoice arrives at the end of the month, the company that launched the campaign has already recovered the revenues and liquidity invested thanks to the sales generated with advertising.
The question is not different. *How much to invest in a Facebook campaign?*

We are now closer, but not quite yet.

You see, unlike stock market investments, a Facebook campaign doesn't need to wait years to bear its fruits. Thanks to the tracking of results, it only takes a few days to see how things are going.

Consequently, you usually start by investing minimum amounts and observe the result. If it's good, you invest more; if it is not good, you return to the design phase of the campaign.

These continuous tests are the soul of online advertising on and off Facebook, and it's good that it is this way. Thanks to these tests, in fact, campaigns are kept running only when they are profitable.

Now let's get into the topic. How does Facebook determine the price you have to pay for your campaign?

The concept of auction

Advertising spaces on Facebook are limited, and are sold to the highest bidder. Behind the scenes, where we do not see, a complex algorithm assigns the available spaces to the various advertisers.

Whenever we see an advertisement on Facebook, we are really looking at the result of a competition between advertisers who have tried to buy it.

Every time our ad appears on someone's feed, we are paying Facebook the price it took to win that space.

As is always the case in auctions, the price of ad visibility is not constant. It varies according to the demand and supply of advertising space.

Budget selection

When we start our Facebook campaign, we will be asked how much we want to invest. We decide it.

We also have two options to choose from:

- **Overall budget.** It indicates how much we want to spend over the life of our campaign;

- **Daily budget.** It indicates how much we want to invest, day by day, to show our ads. Usually it starts with around $15-35 per day, and then increases if the results are good.

Here we don't want to go into very technical details, but in general we advise you to keep in mind the following things.

- Starting with too low of a budget does not provide enough indicative results;
- Starting with a budget that is too high makes you obtain lower performances than those obtained starting from the bottom and gradually increasing.

Manual Bid vs Automatic Bid

Bid means "offer". You can manage your advertisements basically in two ways.

- Letting Facebook optimize your bid in auctions for advertisements;

- By manually setting the price you are willing to pay for each space.

The first option is the automatic bid, the second is the manual bid.

There are also two types of bids to choose from.

- **Bid per click.** It allows you to optimize our offer based on the cost for each click we get on your ad;

- **Bid per impression.** It allows you to optimize your bid for the cost of getting 1,000 views of your ad, regardless of how many people click on it.

Which one to choose from these options? The answer is simple: you have to test.

In any case, it is likely that at first you will set up an automatic bid. After analyzing the data related to the automatic bid, you usually switch to a more optimized manual bid.

On average, consider the following aspects.

- The cost to get 1,000 views of a Facebook ad in the US is $2-3
- The average cost per click is $0.10-0.50

These are not official figures. They are the simple fruit of many years of investment in Facebook ads, and are absolutely first-hand numbers.

Bid vs Action cost

In the previous paragraph we lied to you. There are not only bids per click and per impression. Or rather, there are only the two of them but we can be even more specific in asking Facebook to optimize our campaign.

We can choose to set a maximum cost for achieving a custom goal. We can therefore ask Facebook to respect a maximum cost (e.g. $10 per purchase) and to use this benchmark to establish our maximum cost per click and per impression.

However, never forget the following things.

- **Facebook doesn't work miracles.** If it fails to reach the goal you have set with the budget you make available to it, it will stop showing your campaigns;

- Even if ultimately it is the sales or contacts of interested viewers that interest you, in the first advertising campaigns it is better to choose goals such as clicks and landing page views;

- Often and willingly, the costs of achieving a goal will have significant ups and downs even within a few weeks.

Placement of adverts

Facebook Ads are not only published on Facebook. You can also show your ads on Instagram and on Audience Network. The latter is a set of websites and newspapers that collaborates with Facebook by renting its advertising space.

The choice of positioning is far from irrelevant. In fact, each space has the right format to use, and a recommended type of creativity. If you mix highly effective creativity with flawless targeting, but make a mistake in your choice of placement, you could ruin all other efforts.

Let's take a closer look at the options you have available.

Facebook

The advertising formats available on Facebook are the following.

- **Feed.** Your ad will be shown on the users feed. The most effective creativity in these cases is usually a video, preferably in a square or vertical format;

- **Video carousel**. If your creative is a video, it can be shown in the related video carousel when a user watches any video on Facebook;

- **Messenger:** For some time now, Facebook has allowed us to send sponsored messages within its chat. It normally works well for market research;

- **Sidebar.** Facebook can show your ad in the right column of the site, to reach users who are browsing from desktop;

- **Stories.** They won't be as popular as Instagram's, but Facebook has its own stories too. And we can use them for advertising, especially using videos in strictly vertical format (9:16).

Instagram

Instagram has belonged to Facebook for a long time now, and has entered its advertising space.

On Instagram we have some of the formats already seen on Facebook: feeds, stories and video carousel.

In addition we have a native format called discovery ads. Quite simply, your content will be published in the "Explore" section of Instagram blending very well with non-sponsored content.

In the case of discovery ads, for the best results we recommend using images as a creativity.

Audience Network

Audience Network is a set of websites, applications and mobile games that have partnered up with Facebook and that you can use to display your ads on.

Your ads may appear in different formats.

- **Feed**. Inserted within an article;

- **Rewarded Video.** The user can watch your sponsored video within an application, obtaining in-game rewards in exchange;

- **In-Stream.** Your sponsored video will be played within the application used by the user as an advertisement break.

Audience Network is a little less effective, but also significantly less expensive than premium placements on the users' feed. Depending on the case, it can be the best choice as well as the absolute worst.

Creativity of the ad, which one to choose?

Creativity is the main component of the advertisment. It can be a photo, a video, a photo carousel, or a photo and video carousel.

Facebook, from this point of view, thrives on fashions. Based on how the algorithm of the moment is structured, there are more or less effective "epochs" of creativity.

Without wanting to tell you the whole story of Facebook Ads from its inception, let's jump straight to the creatives that today (and presumably over the next two years) are proving to be most effective.

There are essentially three types of effective creative you can use today.

- **Images with strongly contrasting colors**. These are able to attract the user's attention and entice him to read the ad copy;

- Very short and fast videos, full of cuts and dynamic images that tell the essence of the advertisement in a matter of seconds - typically between 20 and 30 -;

- Very, very long videos - typically over an hour and a half - with a detailed webinar.

In general, there are two schools of thought. That of those who think that creativity should attract the user's attention as much as possible, and that of those who think that it should maximize the amount of information transmitted to the user.

The truth? Both work, depending on the specific situation. And guess what you need to do to find out which is the best one for your products or services? You have to test. Hopefully by now you have understood that testing is the mother of all truths when it comes down to Facebook ads.

Write winning copy

Facebook Ads have become a great new start for this blend of art, science and creativity. Difficult to enclose everything in a few lines, but we will try our best to give you a fresh perspective on the importance of copywriting for Facebook ads.

In general, make sure you write something directly related to the problem your product or service can solve in the first two lines of your listing.

Moving forward, you have three options.

- Let your landing page explain more about what you propose and cut short on the copy;

- Continue your explanation, starting from the problem and going downstream towards the way in which your product or service is able to solve it;

- Talk very deeply about the problem and postpone explaining how your product or service solves it to the landing page.

Without even needing to mention it, the answer to this puzzle are tests.

The art and duty of A/B Testing

We've lost count of the number of times tests have already been brought up in this chapter. Here is a small summary of all the components of your campaign that you must remember to test, several times, to optimize it from time to time.

- Public;
- Placement;
- Budget;
- Bid;
- Creativity;
- Copy.

You don't have to radically change your campaign every time you test something. Otherwise it will be very difficult to understand which variable led to improvements or worsening of performance.

Start by testing different audiences, keeping the other variables the same; continue testing different placements, keeping the audience that performed best and the other variables the same as before.
Then test the budget using the audience and placement that worked best, and so on.

Whenever you take a test, you can also choose to test more than two different options.

In technical jargon, it says you have to do continuous A/B Testing.

The importance of an effective and responsive landing page

The landing page is crucial. First of all, avoid the typical mistake of choosing the site's homepage as your landing page. The landing page must be created specifically, based on the content and message of the advertisement.

To work at its best, it must offer the customer a clear and valuable offer right from the title.

Example: "Remove forehead wrinkles in 90 days or get your money back".

Remember that people have a basic distrust of advertising messages. Attract them by offering a guarantee formula, such as the following.

- Money Back Guarantee
- Free samples
- Free advice before purchasing

Or, even better, build a sales process that does not immediately end with the purchase. For example, offer free information material or a no-obligation first call. Try to bring the customer closer to the purchase slowly, without forcing him too much. Present your offer objectively and in detail, and conclude with a nice call to action.

To promote the effectiveness of your call to action, give the user a reason to act immediately. For example, you can apply the following tactics.

- Offer a timed discount;

- Warn the user that he will no longer be able to perform this action after a certain date

- Show the number of available stocks or appointments left.

In general, put pressure on the user not to postpone the action. This is called "urgency" and is one of the most important social media marketing concepts there are.

By applying the principles explained in this chapter, you are going to create amazing ads from the start, which is something not a lot of social media marketers can say to have done. Remember to test as much as possible and build up the daily budget as good results come in.

If you follow these guidelines, success is almost guaranteed.

Chapter 12

Instagram and Followers

Now that we have discussed Facebook and the impact it can have in an effective social media marketing strategy, it is time to shift our focus to another important social media platform. We are talking about Instagram, the social network based on pictures and stories.

Let's start by answering the first question that people have when they approach this social media platform for the first time. How can you gain more followers and visibility?

It is a question that today makes more and more sense to ask, because Instagram has become one of the most popular social networks in the US and in the world. In our country there are currently about 200 million users, with a prevalent age of less than 30 years. A social network that is very popular among young people and that represents a very effective channel especially for companies capable of communicating through images.

Obviously, the results of good communication on Instagram are obtained if you are able to communicate to a very large pool of people. In other words, if an account is very popular, every post published will reach a large audience and if the content is valid, a very high level of engagement will be obtained. A large number of followers means having an audience that is always ready to receive the messages shared and therefore to give value to the marketing communication efforts that the company makes. Obviously having a large number of followers alone does not necessarily lead to economic results, but it is impossible not to recognize that it is a good starting point towards monetization.

In general, having a lot of followers means not being forced to continually spend money and time on advertising to give visibility to a post. A good post that organically reaches a large sample of users representing its audience of potential customers can trigger word of mouth, in the form of mentions or shares. This quickly leads to a significant spread of the message and therefore to a great reputation without financial investments in addition to those related to the creation and production of the content.

What are the most valid ways to increase the number of followers on Instagram? It can be said right away that the shortcut is advertising. Investing in advertising with quality, very engaging and well aimed at a target audience content, is the best way to gain followers. Obviously, this method requires an upfront payment, which in some cases can even be considerable for small companies or personal brands. While many large companies have no difficulty in regularly investing large sums of money in social media advertising, the same cannot be said for smaller companies. While it is advisable from time to time to launch advertising campaigns on Instagram, it is also clear that this cannot be the only method to achieve positive results on this social network.

So here is a short guide to increase followers on Instagram by exploiting only the non-paid features offered by the platform.

1. Curate your profile information

When a user finds a post interesting, he often wants to know who has published it and will therefore check the account. At that point he will start browsing through the images, but he will also look for information in the bio and in the few institutional areas that Instagram makes available to users to introduce themselves. If he finds everything interesting and well set up, the chances of him deciding to become a follower will increase considerably.

It is therefore essential to take the time to carefully define every single significant part of the profile. Do not skip this first step as it is the starting point for more complex Instagram marketing strategies.

2. Publish quality images

At the base of any activity that can be carried out in Instagram is the quality of the images that are published. All images must be expressive, aesthetically pleasing and as original as possible. To obtain excellent results it is good to be able to equip yourself with professional image editing and shooting tools, in order to produce visual content of high aesthetic value. It is also advisable to have graphic and photo editing skills, in order to be able to edit the images and make them more captivating and engaging.

Instagram itself provides a certain number of filters that can be used in order to facilitate the editing process, but alone they cannot work miracles. In fact, to be successful, the starting photo has to be high quality. By now the most popular images are those that have the greatest aesthetic impact and users can immediately distinguish amateur content from the more artistic and qualitative pictures. Only the latter will be able to win attention to the point of inducing users to follow the account that published them, thus increasing the number of followers.

3. Exploit the power of captions

A photo's caption isn't the first thing you notice in a post. But often it is the one that gives meaning to the image, leading the user to stop and think. A good caption fixes the emotion aroused by the photo, transforming it into a more structured concept.

The best captions are the witty and funny ones, but also those that make users reflect on a specific topic, those that ask a question or propose to do some specific action, such as supporting a humanitarian cause or deepening a particular topic. The more engaged a user is, the more likely they are to become a follower.

4. Publish content frequently and regularly

The quality of the photos published is essential, but it is not enough to reach high number of followers. You also need to post content at a high frequency and on a regular basis. The ideal is to post images twice a day, but if you can't do that, you have to keep the pace of one post a day. In this way, users will more easily come into contact with the published content and the chances of getting new followers will multiply.

To have this consistency in the publication it is essential to define a real editorial plan, as we explained in a previous chapter. In fact, if every time you try to publish a picture you have to create it from scratch, and after a certain period of greater enthusiasm you will lose much of the initial motivation and you will end up not posting anymore. If, on the other hand, you do a well-structured job of weekly or even monthly planning, the effort in producing the content will only take place the first time, then you will only have to deal with posting the pictures. It must also be said that if the contents are planned ahead, there will be greater coherence in your profile and a more compact and targeted communication. Users will appreciate and be more inclined to become followers if they see consistency in what you are posting.

5. Make wise use of hashtags

Hashtags on Instagram are really the engine of the entire platform. In fact, the social network was designed to host up to thirty hashtags in each post and although it is not the case to exploit all the characters available, there is no doubt that success on the platform in terms of acquiring followers requires a wide use of this tool. Hashtags are the way through which users who are not already followers can find your posts. For this purpose, before starting to post, it is essential to conduct a research on the trending and most used hashtags among those most relevant to the content you want to publish, in order to reach the users potentially most interested in those topics.

6. Engage with other users

To increase the number of followers on Instagram, you need to point out your presence not only through your own content, but also by commenting on the posts of other users.

The tip we want to give you is the following.

Open the feed of a hashtag relevant to your content - or start following the most interesting ones - and when you see interesting posts give them a like. The users who posted them will notice your likes and will easily check out your profile. By repeating these actions on their posts, the chances that many users will start following you will be very high.

An even more effective way is to comment on their photos. In fact, in this way in addition to making yourself visible, you will open a dialogue with them, which will make them even more involved and kindly disposed towards you. Yet another way is to mention them in your posts. Users will receive free visibility and will be willing to reciprocate by starting to follow you. In some cases it may also be useful to send direct messages to some particularly active and interesting users. Obviously in this case an interesting, engaging, non-trivial message will have to be crafted, you don't want to be annoying. Therefore, do not send promotional or spammy messages, as they are the perfect way to lose followers over time.

7. Establish a solid relationship with influencers

A great way to get noticed is to go in search of the most influential users and interact with them. In fact, if you manage to attract the attention of the right influencer and make him passionate about your pictures and what you communicate to the public, you can benefit from visibility and a considerable brand awareness in return. Influencers in fact exerts a strong involvement towards their followers, who often tend to imitate their behaviors and tastes. If the influencer begins to show interest in a certain brand, it is very likely that a significant share of his followers will do the same. For you this interest will translate into new followers and potential customers.

Obviously, the biggest challenge is to get influencers to mention you and promote your page. A good influencer marketing policy must be put in place in this case. First of all, good relationships must be established with influencers by following their content and giving them likes and comments. In this way, their ego will be leveraged, leading them to look at your brand with more attention and availability. They can then be contacted directly in order to offer remuneration in exchange for the mention of your brand or your products. Micro-influencers can also be satisfied with some free products, the bigger ones will ask for a check as well. If the requested amount is not too expensive or disproportionate to the visibility they can give you, it is absolutely worth it to accept the collaboration.

8. Track users' followers

When you follow a user, they are notified and often reciprocate with a followback. So, to increase your followers, a good way is to start following those users you want to have among your fans.

The problem is that if you follow too many users while there are few who reciprocate, you run the risk of having a high number of following and a low number of followers, which is not very positive in the eyes of the public. When you realize that a certain user has not given the follow back it can be advantageous to stop following him. On the other hand, if you receive a follow from a target user, it is better to follow him to consolidate the relationship and reduce the risk of unfollowing. Basically it is advisable to continuously monitor the flow of followers, using for example applications such as Unfollower Stats or Followers & Likes Tracker for Instagram. These tools are able to monitor in real time the behavior of users in relation to their account and give the opportunity to quickly manage the following. unfollows and follow backs.

9. Use stories in the right way

Stories are extremely popular on Instagram. Many users prefer them to regular posts. Publishing good stories means increasing the chances of being noticed by users, with the effect of leading them to become followers.

To make the most of the expressive power of stories, you must make use of stickers adapting them to the content you want to propose. Furthermore, many of the stickers allow you to stimulate users to interact with the content, increasing the level of engagement and arousing positive emotions, which easily lead to transforming an occasional user into a follower.

If your company or personal brand do not use Instagram stories, we warmly advise you to start implementing them in your social media marketing strategies. They are an extremely powerful tool.

10.   Advertise posts that have generated the most interest

A post that has collected more interactions than the average is obviously a post that has great potential and is highly appreciated by your followers. In this case, investing a small budget in advertising is a good decision. The promotion will allow it to be shown to a wider audience than the one reachable organically through the normal functioning of Instagram algorithms.

If you already have a considerable number of followers that are very targeted and quite similar in characteristics and interests, you can choose to entrust the definition of the target audience to the advertising algorithm. Instagram will identify the characteristic traits of the audience that normally follows your profile and will track down other similar users. If, on the other hand, you have few followers, it is better to create an audience with characteristics assigned based on interests, age class and other parameters that can better target advertising exposure. You can do this by following the steps explained in the chapter dedicated to Facebook ads.

Chapter 13

How to Generate More Sales Using Instagram

Now that we have discussed how to gain more followers, it is time to look at things from a different perspective. In fact, the goal of this book is to teach you how to monetize users' attention. Therefore, we have decided to dedicate this chapter to the strategies you can implement to generate more sales using Instagram.

Let's get right into it.

To improve the performance and increase sales Instagram can be a valuable ally. It is necessary to study a very specific strategy of building the brand and caring for the relationship with customers. Once you have laid out the strategy, Instagram can be an excellent tool to turn attention into sales.

According to a research presented by Yotpo, about 30% of Instagram users made an online purchase after seeing the product in some photos published on the social network. Furthemore, the engagement rate of this type of customer is about 58 times higher than what normally you can have on Facebook.

Furthermore, on Instagram the user tends to watch a very high number of posts, which on Facebook is now more limited. It is therefore not surprising that brands and companies see Instagram as a valid ally. But what measures need to be implemented to generate sales on a regular basis? Are there better strategies than others to support the launch of an online store and to increase its visibility and sales?

Here are some techniques you should follow if you want to use Instagram to sell your products or services.

Create a business account

Instagram offers its users a rich amount of functions, but it allows companies to obtain even wider operational results, provided they open a real business account. Configuring it is very easy and it only takes a few minutes. In the settings of your profile you find the "Switch to a company account" button and from here you just need to follow the instructions to complete the upgrade.

The advantages of a business profile are numerous. First of all, you can enter specific information concerning the company, such as opening hours, address, telephone number and email. It is also possible to access a number of statistics regarding the performance of stories and posts, but also regarding the behavior of followers.

All this information allows you to improve the quality of the published content and thus create a better relationship with users, making it more likely that they will respond positively when they are offered something to buy on your online store.

Use a creative brand image

The first step to take before starting to communicate on Instagram is to build the brand image. Green light therefore to graphic experimentations for the creation of a logo and even fonts and colors that are recognizable and unique. What strikes the attention of users the most in this social network is the authenticity and naturalness of the images presented.

In the first era of Instagram the most effective and most appreciated images were those taken spontaneously, which portrayed situations photographed using the mobile phone directly. But now, in the phase of full maturity of the social network, you can successfully publish any beautiful image capable of expressing a strong and engaging content on an emotional level.

As we have seen in the previous chapter, the only condition is that there is good coherence and that all images communicate a universe of content that can be traced back to the well-recognizable and characterized brand.

An original and particular brand, with a strong image, will accentuate the attention paid by the public and will increase interest in visiting the e-commerce site to discover the products or services offered.

Focus on posting valuable content

On Instagram the first temptation is to post content that you know it has performed well in the past. A kitten or a stunning photo can certainly attract more likes, but they rarely communicate something that gives real value to the users.

On the other hand, in order to simplify the creation of new content and to immediately showcase customers their products, companies tend to publish mainly posts with images of products that seem to have been extracted directly from pre-packaged catalogs. This is also a wrong choice, because only in a few cases the Instagram user is attracted to this type of photo. It is much better to contextualize the products trying to capture them in contexts of real use or in small episodes that recall a potentially real narrative.

A good formula for success is to create images in which you see people using the products and enjoying them. In this way the potential buyer will feel encouraged to believe that other consumers really like the product. Obviously, this will push him to purchase the product.

In general, the most effective posts are those that suggest the idea of a narrative, of a real event described in a single image. Another type of post that works wonders are pictures that directly engage with users, involving them with questions or urging them to do something specific.

Static product images may also be posted from time to time, but the use of this type of image should not exceed 20% of all published posts. This type of content can also have a particular promotion as its description, such as a discount or zero shipping costs. In this way it will be easy to direct many users who appreciate the brand and follow it regularly to visit the e-commerce site.

Using Stories Effectively

Another trick is to use stories appropriately. Unlike standard posts, stories always have the flavor of a "hit and run" content, which is something very emotional and at the same time ephemeral and instantaneous. For this reason, if you want to promote your e-commerce using stories, you have to tailor your strategy accordingly.

This means you have to avoid static product presentations, which in stories can really bore users. The best way is to propose promotions on the go, with a link that allows users to buy immediately. In other words you have to make the purchasing process as frictionless as possible.

Alternatively, stories can be very effective for increasing brand awareness through short highly emotional videos, messages from satisfied customers, micro-stories about the brand, the company or the use of the products and very short videos that help to understand the advantages deriving from the purchase of your product or service.

Some stickers can help spice up the story content. Among the most valid one, we find the following.

- **Countdown**. It allows you to insert a timer in the Story in order to highlight that a particular promotion is about to end.
- **Questions**. This sticker allows users to ask questions about the content of the Story.

- **Survey**. It allows you to ask questions with closed answers. For instance, if the story showcases two products, you can do a survey asking which of the two users like more.

The insertion of a sticker increases the likelihood that users interact with the story, thus helping to increase interest and attention to the content you post. If you do not have the possibility to insert a link because you have not reached 10,000 followers yet, it is always advisable to insert a text that invites users to click the link in bio.

Frequency of publication

The average life of an Instagram post is about 20 hours. Therefore, it is ideal to publish one picture per day. However, it must be said that the frequency of posts must be decided after a careful study of the competitors and the habits of users who are most likely interested in the niche you are in.

Also pay attention to the type of content you publish. In fact, depending on the time of the year, or even the week, it may be more appropriate to choose certain images rather than others. A precise publication plan not based on improvisation can allow you to appropriately choose which products and content to promote at the most convenient moment. This is why the editorial plan is such a great tool at your disposal and why we are focusing on it so much during this book.

Specially designed links

Inserting links in Instagram posts is currently not an available feature. This could be a problem if you do not know how to overcome it, but it can be easily solved thanks to a well thought out communication plan.

For this purpose, the first thing to focus on is the biography in which you can insert the link to your site. If you are promoting a particular product it is advisable to insert the link to the page of said product.

In practice, every time you promote a certain product, you should immediately update the link in the bio, in order to give users the opportunity to check it out immediately. Completing a posted image with a call to action referring to the link in the bio is a good way to generate traffic to your online store.

Choose the best hashtags

Another aspect to consider are hashtags. They are not only useful to give context to posts, but above all to intercept a pool of users that is as wide and as interested as possible. The choice of hashtags must be made following precise criteria, keeping in mind that the ideal number on Instagram is between 9 and 12 even if it is possible to insert up to 30 hashtags.

Space for user's engagement

If you have an online store it is useful to have customers' reviews and feedback. For this purpose you can consider the idea of inviting those who have already purchased a product to take photos and post them on Instagram with a dedicated hashtag, perhaps in exchange for a coupon code on their next purchase.

More simply, customers can be encouraged to have their say about a product or something about the brand through explicit questions, linked to some particular images. As a consequence, comments and likes will increase, making it more likely that the next posts will be seen again by those users who have interacted with the first one.

To take full advantage of these pictures it is even possible to mention their creators on the site along with the reviews. In this way it will be possible to create a social proof that can entice other customers to buy it.

Set up and leverage the "Shopping on Instagram" feature
Shopping on Instagram is a recently introduced feature to allow businesses that have an e-commerce to display products directly on Instagram. The

function allows you to configure a catalog of products so that you can mention them directly within your posts or stories using specific tags or stickers.

In practice, after creating a post, before publishing it you can tap the "Tag products" button to add the reference to one or more products in your catalog to the post. Once the Shopping function is enabled, it will also be possible to tag products even in posts already published. Furthermore in stories the products can be tagged using a special sticker.

When users click on a tag referring to a product in a post or a sticker related to the product in a story, they will be directed directly to another page that presents the description of the product. On this page they will find an image, a description and the cost of the product together with a link that points directly to the product sheet on your e-commerce site, where they can complete the purchase.

We have used this feature pretty extensively and we can say that it can yield amazing results if used appropriately.

Analysis and control of results

Last but not least, you must always define KPIs and measure the results of the actions you take. In fact, only in this way will you know if the activities on Instagram aimed at increasing e-commerce sales have worked or not.

To discover which KPIs are the most crucial ones you can go back to chapter 7.

Make use of Instagram Checkout when available

Instagram Checkout is a payment system that is revolutionizing the world of online sales and Instagram is the first social network that makes it possible to sell directly on its platform. In this way, the user can take advantage of an easy, fast and secure virtual customer experience guaranteeing the company or personal brand direct economic returns.

The goal of Instagram Checkout is to capture the user's attention through images. Instagram through the technique of feeds, stories and visual storytelling offers the possibility to communicate your product or service in the best possible way, and the Checkout function is the perfect way to end the consumer's process with the purchase inside of the platform.

The posts from which users can make purchases with Instagram Checkout are those found in the "Explore" section under the "Shopping" category. By clicking on the tag, a label appears on the purchasable product, with information about the name and its price.

For now, the possibility to purchase and pay via the "Checkout on Instagram" button without referring to external sites is only active in organic posts, in stories and in the "Explore" tab. In fact, at the moment the feature has been released in beta. Instagram still considers it an experiment for a few privileged companies, but our opinion is it will not take long before this feature will be made available to every business or personal brand.

For now, in-app purchase is only available to users living in the United States and has been reserved for a limited number of brands and companies including Nike, Adidas, H&M, Zara, Michael Kors, Burberry,

Dior, Prada and MAC Cosmetics. These companies will have to pay a percentage on each purchase for the service to Instagram but neither the figures nor the methods have been communicated yet.

In any case, Checkout is proof that Zuckerberg and associates are increasingly aiming directly at introducing electronic commerce systems on Instagram and Facebook in which affiliated companies can sell their products directly maximizing earnings.

Now you should have a clear understanding of how to generate sales using Instagram. We have almost reached the end of our discussion about this social media, but before moving on it is important to talk about a recent change and what it means for your business. The next chapter will tell you everything there is to know about the disappearance of the number of likes.

Chapter 14

No More Likes

Recently, Instagram decided to stop displaying the number of likes under photos. This is a first-time event in social media's history and it is safe to say nothing will ever be the same now. Do not worry, though, the impact on your social media marketing strategy is minimal, but there are a few things to know about this topic.

Let's try to understand why Zuckerberg decided to make this change.

More quality, less quantity. This, in summary, is the message that Instagram wants to convey to its users. Under each post the number of likes will no longer be visible. In fact, from a few months ago the user can only see the likes of followers under each post without being able to trace the total number of likes. Only the owner of the account who published the post will therefore have access to the actual number of likes.

The reasons for this choice

Tara Hopkins, Head of Public Policy EMEA at Instagram expressed herself pretty clearly. This is her statement.

> *"We want to help people focus their attention on photos and videos shared and not on the number of likes they receive. We want Instagram to be a space where everyone can feel free to express themselves. We are conducting several tests in multiple countries to understand directly from the community of all our users how this novelty can improve their experience on Instagram".*

In other words, without the appearance of a post's "success", users will be more stimulated to share more authentic content without seeking immediate and in some cases almost forced approval from followers.

The consequences of this choice

This is a radical change of course, which will entail not indifferent consequences, both positive and negative. The subjects most interested in this change are certainly those who had so far used Instagram as a business tool, such as companies and influencers. In short, a double-edged sword for those who had so far focused heavily on "hearts" to increase their user base.

Those who can benefit from this novelty, on the other hand, are certainly small companies or mid-range influencers on the "launch pad", who will be able to exploit the potential of Instagram without the constraint of the number of likes of the various posts.

Do not forget that the Instagram algorithm will still be able to detect the approval rating of an image that will be automatically included among the recommended or most relevant posts. Furthermore, the number of followers of the single account will remain visible, so as not to excessively penalize those who have created and strengthened an authentic brand during these years.

The consequences for hashtags and dedicated apps

What role will hashtags and apps created to increase likes now have?

As for hashtags, they will probably be used more wisely, in line with the nature of the single post published, without being used disproportionately at the cost of desperately reaching a certain number of hearts.

The apps, on the other hand, will have an almost logical and natural decline, because users will be less stimulated to accumulate fictitious likes, since the numbers will not be visible and will try to compensate by guaranteeing a higher quality of the published content.

Between psychology and technology

The experiment to not display the number of likes had already been announced by Instagram in April during F8, the annual meeting of the developers of the Facebook group. Back then, however, the test was limited to Canada while now it extends to the entire world.

One of the reasons that led to the experimentation and introduction of this novelty is the fight against "like addiction", a psychological phenomenon that is intertwined with the world of social networks.

According to research by Kaspersky (a Russian company specializing in the development of computer security software), 61% of the users interviewed said they were on social media to feel better, but 57% confessed that they could not find what they wanted to see. These are scary data if you ask us. Furthermore, only 31% did not care about the number of "likes" received when publishing a post while 24% of men and 17% of women even got angry if they didn't receive the attention adequate to their initial expectations.

Therefore, the goal is to focus more on authentic values, relationships and the enhancement of quality content. Being yourself, leaving no room for cyberbullying caused by envy and confrontation is the final goal of this change. If the novelty will collect favorable opinions during the next few months it could also be applied to other social networks as well. We feel that Facebook is going to be next.

A strategic choice

There is no doubt that the goal of Zuckerberg and his companions is to turn all their social networks into slot machines. The life cycle of the Instagram product has just entered the phase in which they must aim to consolidate all the obtainable economic results. In other words, the goal is to apply all tactics to maximize the use of any function by ordinary users and companies.

As we said, the elimination of likes aims precisely to give a slap to the influencers, who so far have continued to gain prestige and revenues by exploiting the effects of the social proof obtained thanks to fake followers and likes. The higher the number of likes, the greater the interest of companies to pay to have brands and products mentioned by the influencer. With the visibility of likes fading, it becomes more difficult for influencers to show their strength, so it is not unlikely that in the near future the Instagram team will launch a new paid function dedicated to influencers. We think it will allow them to show the value of a post in terms of results obtained or to guarantee the success of engagement in a more secure way through specific advertising formulas.

Our opinion is that this change does not have negative effects on those that have an effective social media marketing strategy in place. If you follow the guidelines of this book, minor changes like this one will not impact your profitability. On the contrary, if you decide to go all-in on tricks and shady tactics your entire business could collapse in a matter of seconds. We hope you know which way is the one to follow.

Chapter 15

TikTok

We have talked about the importance of Instagram and Facebook in a social media marketing strategy. However, there is one social media that is becoming more and more famous and that could help you increase sales and brand awareness if used correctly. We are talking about TikTok.

In this period, TikTok is the most discussed social media of the moment. First of all for its usage statistics, which are actually impressive.

The public in the US who is interested in using the app is predominantly young, mostly belonging to generation Z. In this context, TikTok can be successful in a digital marketing plan aimed precisely at a population under the age of 25.

The reasons for the amazing success of this social network are numerous and closely linked to the type of operation it allows to do.

The prospects offered to marketers are interesting, but it must be kept in mind that the very young audience is currently the most refractory and distrustful of any message that has the clear goal of advertising.

Usage data worldwide

Worldwide TikTok is available in 155 countries and 75 languages. It currently has around 2 billion active users, with more than 2,5 billion downloads in summer 2020. It is the most downloaded app in the Apple App Store, while it is third in Google Play after WhatsApp and Facebook Messenger.

The geographical areas in which the use of TikTok is the highest are Southeast Asia, in particular in China, India, Japan, Indonesia, Malaysia, Thailand, Vietnam and Cambodia. In particular, in India alone, active users are more than 120 million, while in China, the country where the app was born, there are more than 400 million active users. In the USA there are currently more than 100 million active users and numbers are increasing rapidly, even with the famous issues regarding a possible ban.

Users' behavior

The most peculiar feature of TikTok is that it generates a continuous and tendentially compulsive use. In fact, 90% of TikTok users use the app daily, for an average daily use time of 52 minutes.

Furthermore, TikTok can count on a pretty significant number of creators compared to its total users. In fact, 55% of TikTok accounts post videos on a regular basis. This is a number in contrast to the average of "creatives" in the various social networks that usually do not exceed 30% of the total accounts.

In other words, only one in three users in all social networks is inclined to publish new content of their own creation, while in TikTok one in two users actively participates in the creation flow of new videos. The effect of this trend is that an average of 236 videos per minute are uploaded on the platform. Another significant fact is that TikTok currently has the highest engagement rate among all social media, further proof that the app users are the most active of all social platforms.

The reasons for the success

What are the reasons that led TikTok to such rapid and extraordinary success? Obviously it is impossible to definitively and categorically identify the driving aspects that lead users to fall in love with this app, but certainly there are four specific factors that at this moment assign TikTok the title of most used social media in the world.

In the following pages we take these factors into consideration.

Simple and direct storytelling

TikTok consists of short videos, which can be uploaded directly from your smartphone or tablet. Instinctively, those who publish a video know that they must create a short narrative and this makes the creation of the content more stimulating and engaging.

Unlike a simple image, a video requires the construction of a real story, which must have its own development and its own personality. Although making a video is more challenging than taking a simple picture, the degrees of freedom are much greater and you can tell a moment of your life, an idea or an event in a much broader and more creative way.

The average shortness of TikTok videos makes this process much more basic and simplified than what is expected on YouTube. If in the latter a good video is considered one that is several minutes long and has a very accurate aesthetic and very detailed content, on TikTok the video portrays a simple moment. You just need to have the right idea and in 10 seconds you can have it published online.

Users are the main characters

TikTok users use the app to record videos of themselves. From this point of view, the user is always the main protagonist. In many ways, TikTok videos are an evolution of selfies. In fact, they are able to represent the person in his dynamism, in his daily life and in his full reality and authenticity.

In a few seconds a user is able to tell who he is, express salient traits of his character or share an opinion. But above all the user can show itself in a more engaging and articulated way than with a simple image.

Expressive force

A video is more complex than an image and requires more attention to be recorded, but when it is done well it multiplies the communicative power of any idea. Those who produce a video know that they can take advantage of a richness of expression and a level of engagement much higher than the average of online content.

And if the video, as in the case of those published on TikTok, is by its nature short and concise, its emotional intensity is even greater. In general, videos are able to initiate many more interactions than a simple image or text, because the emotional impact of a video sequence is very high, with the consequence that the stimulus to express a comment or even just to give a like is irresistible.

User friendly

TikTok is an app designed to work on mobile only. Its perfect integration with this type of device is ideal for young people, more inclined to the continuous use of smartphones to get in touch and communicate with friends and acquaintances.

Generation Z has found in this social network the ideal dimension to represent themselves and a very powerful way to communicate, precisely because it exploits the potential of the latest generation mobile phones to the maximum.

Current marketing opportunities

Marketing communication on TikTok is now easier than ever, thanks to the launch of the new ad creation management platform, which allows marketers to schedule their advertisements without requiring the intermediation of TikTok staff.

Obviously, the audience that can be reached is the one between the ages of 15 and 24. At the moment it may not be convenient to insert TikTok in a social media marketing plan aimed at an audience of young adults or over 35. On the contrary, if you aim at the Z generation it is necessary to find a way to develop advertising plans on TikTok as well.

On TikTok, users expect communication that is extremely agile and original, personal and direct, impressive and engaging to the highest degree. All features that most of the commercials designed for television and other social media do not possess very often.

On the contrary, marketing creatives must think totally socially and produce video messages capable of talking to users. They must seek to build a relationship, they have to be original and above all short and fresh. TikTok audiences must feel that the video content in advertising was invented specifically for the platform and that it is unique, even if you are using it on Instagram and Facebook as well.

If TikTok continues to broaden its audience, advertisers will have to thoroughly study and become much more accustomed to the language of this platform.

The beauty of the current situation on TikTok is that attention is ridiculously underpriced. Taking this social media into consideration is a must for every marketer that wants to stay ahead of competition. We highly suggest you start looking into TikTok and try it out a little bit by yourself. In fact, this is always the best way to get started on a new social network and collect the first feedback.

Chapter 16

TikTok's Algorithm

In the previous chapter we gave you a general introduction on how TikTok works and why you should take it into consideration when developing your social media marketing strategy.

In this chapter, we are going to dive a bit deeper and tell you how its algorithm works. Knowing what happens behind the scenes once you upload a video is fundamental to make the most out of this platform.

Recommendation algorithms are very important for a social network, because they determine the quality of engagement, which is the time that each user dedicates to the app. The TikTok algorithm is famous in the world of technology for the accuracy of the recommendations it can give. Eugene Wei, an

American entrepreneur and analyst, wrote this on his personal blog at the beginning of August.

"Before TikTok, I would have said that YouTube had the best algorithm in the video industry, but compared to that of TikTok, the algorithm of YouTube seems rudimentary".

The TikTok algorithm works like this. The first time a person accesses the social network, the system asks him to select some categories of interest, for example "animals" and "travel", on the basis of which to start the recommendations. At that point, the algorithm shows the user eight initial videos, and then another eight depending on how the user behaves with the first batch. To understand whether you like a video or not, the algorithm uses a series of criteria, including interactions, clicks on hashtags, viewing duration and the use of certain filters. The algorithm also takes into account other data, such as the user's language, his country of origin and the type of telephone used.

Based on the information collected, the algorithm begins to show the user videos similar to those they have already liked. To understand if the new videos correspond to the user's tastes, the algorithm uses parameters such as the written content of the posts, hashtags, sounds and songs.

Furthermore, once it begins to get an idea of what the user likes, the algorithm categorizes the user into one or more categories of interest. A user can be identified as belonging to a cluster of lovers of basketball, opera or horse riding. At the same time, all videos are categorized within clusters, and the algorithm creates associations based on the "proximity" between user clusters and content clusters. This means that users classified as horse lovers will be able to see both videos of the "horse riding" cluster and videos that other users in their own cluster have enjoyed.

TikTok states that to make this association between videos and users it uses artificial intelligence but does not explain precisely how it implements it. The functioning of TikTok's artificial intelligence is its main secret, and the company does not want to reveal it. Unfortunately, we do not know this secret.

TikTok also has systems in place to understand if the user does not like a video. In fact, the algorithm tries not to show two videos in a row with the same song or created by the same person, and from time to time tries to offer the user videos that do not exactly correspond to his tastes, to make him discover new things. Despite this, TikTok recognizes that its algorithm can lead to the creation of "filter bubbles". A filter bubble is a recommendation system that continuously shows videos that are always homogeneous in terms of themes and contents and always adhering to user preferences. We find this practice extremely dangerous for users' minds.

TikTok announced in July that it would make public some features of its algorithm, to show transparency and accountability. In this regard, Michael Beckerman, vice president of TikTok with responsibility for public relations in the United States, stated that TikTok is "a company born two years ago that has to deal with the expectations of a ten-year-old company".

TikTok's algorithm is also the reason why the US does not like it very much. In early August, Donald Trump signed an executive order that TikTok must sell all of its local business to an American company to avoid being banned to users in the US. Trump's motivation is that TikTok is owned by ByteDance, a Chinese company based in Beijing, and therefore constitutes a national security threat. Trump gave TikTok until mid-November to find a buyer, but the negotiations with Microsoft and Oracle were complicated by the fact that ByteDance does not want to give up the formula of his algorithm. In addition, in early September, the Chinese government approved new restrictions that prevent local companies from exporting certain technologies, including those involving artificial intelligence making it even more difficult for TikTok to follow Trump's guidelines.

We rarely express our opinion in our books, but we feel we would be dishonest if we did not state very clearly that to us TikTok represents a danger to human consciousness. We have spent hours trying each feature it has to offer and the amount of content users are exposed to is exaggerate.

If you are a TikTok user, we warmly advise you to limit your daily use. On the other hand, if you are a social media marketer you can definitely take advantage of the amount of popularity the platform has right now.

Chapter 17

Twitter and Sales: a Basic Introduction

The third social media platform we are going to talk about is Twitter. In particular, let's focus on how to increase your potential customers and sales using this old but still amazing social network.

Increasing e-commerce sales through social media is much more than a possibility, as we have seen during the course of this book. Even the much mistreated Twitter can give satisfaction in this sense. In fact, we want to make clear that each social media can generate interesting results, if you know how to use them properly.

Let's start by looking at some good practices to get started in the right way.

1. Account creation and optimization

First of all you need to work on your account to make it stand out as much as possible. From the colors of the cover and profile photos to the name of your account, everything must talk about you and your e-commerce. Building a precise identity is essential in order to always be recognized and recognizable. You should try to write a description that is rich in keywords and hashtags relevant to your niche. In this way, anyone who comes across your account will be able to get a clearer idea of who you are and what you sell even without visiting the site.

2. Research and interact with your followers

Gathering followers can be a very long and somewhat frustrating process on Twitter. Accounts often grow slowly and many underestimate the platform for this. However, this is a job that must be done with care and method, also through the use of lists, contacts of our competitors and a wise use of the search bar made available by the social network itself.

Once we have created our pool of loyal users, let's not leave them in a corner, but let's start talking to them by engaging with them directly through mentions.

3. Tweet a lot during the day

Twitter is the social network of instant thoughts and as such every user is constantly inundated with tweets, images and messages. The only way to be able to overcome this "noise" and get noticed by your customers and potential clients is to tweet a lot during the day. Obviously it is good to make sure that the message is not always the same. Instead, you should try to take advantage of the opportunity to experiment with new forms and ideas of communication in order to intercept the tastes of all potentially interested users.

4. Monitor Twitter analytics

Twitter analytics is a very useful tool for companies and professionals who use Twitter to work and the same is true for those who have a personal brand or online store. After an initial test period, in fact, it will be the data collected by this tool that will tell you whether you are doing a good job or not, allowing you to adjust the shot if necessary.

Before diving deeper into Twitter Ads, which are the main advertising feature of Twitter, we need to talk about its algorithm. The next chapter is going to tell you everything you need to know about it.

Chapter 18

Twitter and Its Algorithm

The functioning of the Twitter timeline algorithm has been a subject of discussion for a long time, especially among those who intended to denigrate it and find a reason for its failure. Now it is the social network itself to provide an answer and some indiscretion on the future of how its timeline works.

The rationale behind positioning tweets in the timeline was pretty simple. In fact, it was a chronological criterion that sorted the tweets of people being followed from most recent to oldest.

The chronological criterion can be interesting in order to be constantly updated on the latest news and events in the world. Think of the Trends that for many users are really an obsession. In fact, there are many users who try to exploit the waves of trends to ensure that their tweet gets greater visibility. But what was initially the peculiarity of Twitter soon showed its limits. In fact, if it could be fun and useful to receive updates in real time, when the number of users began to increase with it, the user experience began to decrease in terms of quality. Unless you were always connected and attentive, it was clear that being able to manage the large amount of data and information was really too much.

For this reason, the social network has decided to change the algorithm of its timeline and to offer a series of tools to users to categorize tweets. Thanks to the lists, it is possible to bring together in one place the accounts that are most interesting to you without having to worry too much to find them in the sea of tweets.

But Twitter has also made changes to its algorithm. This is not a novelty out of the ordinary but it can be interesting to know them to increase your chances of success. In particular, each tweet as well as based on the chronological criterion is ordered according to the score earned, which is calculated essentially taking into account the following three factors.

- **The tweet.** In particular, this considers the range, the interactions and the presence or absence of multimedia content.

- **The author of the tweet.** The more interactions with the author, the more the friendship with the user will be perceived as strong and the higher the score of the tweet will be.

- **The user.** This mainly considers what his behavior
  is and what his interests are.

Knowing how the algorithm works means you can take advantage of it in your social media marketing strategy. Like we suggested for TikTok, we encourage you to test a bit by yourself how Twitter works, before continuing reading this book.

Chapter 19

Twitter Ads

As with Facebook, Twitter also provides companies with various solutions for social media marketing.

Twitter ads allow companies to connect their business to people's conversations, at the right times and in the right contexts, and allow you to amplify the reach of messages compared to "organic" tweets, creating a strong bond even with the base of existing followers. Even on Twitter the ads are displayed among tweets posted by users, and are similar in format for the possibility of liking, retweeting and replying to standard tweets. They differ in that they are labeled as "sponsored".

This platform, in its operating logic, is similar to Facebook Ads; it differs, however, as the ads are more focused on establishing relationships and obtaining greater customer engagement, while not neglecting any conversions in terms of sales, reservations, registrations and downloads.

How to set up an advertising campaign with Twitter Ads

Although the platform can be a solution that reaches a "global" audience, Twitter Ads can also allow local companies to reach the target of its territory.

So let's see how a local company can set up an advertising campaign on Twitter step by step.

Setting the goal

Not too long ago Twitter introduced a feature similar to that of Facebook Ads Management, and which was previously called "Campaign Selector", which allows you to choose the advertising goal to be achieved when starting a new advertising campaign. Each goal has specific and different functionalities. In our case of a local business, the goals could be "Clicks to the website or conversions" or "Interactions with tweets".

Budget setting

Once the goal has been selected, you will be directed to the choice of the name of the campaign, as well as to the payment method settings and the start and end date of the campaign. You will also select the amount of budget, which can be daily or total. We can suggest to Twitter that we have a certain amount of money available and that it must not exceed it. In our opinion, this is useful if you have spending constraints and, on the other hand, are not able to define the date on which the campaign will end.

Ad group and bid strategy

After setting the name, budget and dates, you will create your first ad group, giving it a name and choosing a start and end date, if you don't want it to start and end at the same time as the entire campaign.

Within the same section you can choose the bidding strategy with which to participate in advertising auctions for the publication of ads and check your level of spending. Selecting a specific offer and its value is a strategic choice that should not be underestimated, as it represents the value you give to that particular advert, sponsored product or service. Therefore, the offer is conditioned by the marketing goals that you have set for yourselves. For click and conversion goals, which is the goal we always recommend using on Twitter, there are three bidding options. These are the following.

- **Automatic offer**. With this type of option you let Twitter decide the advertising offer. It will allow Twitter to automatically optimize the results based on the chosen goal at the lowest possible price.

- **Target cost.** With this type of option you will select a target value that represents the average daily cost around which the platform will have to follow to obtain conversions (recommended for campaigns where the budget is growing over time).

- **Maximum bid.** With this type of option you will select the maximum value that Twitter will not have to exceed to get as many results as possible. As you will discover by testing, in most cases you will spend less than what you have indicated.

Target selection

In this section you will define the audience to reach. The company will set a series of demographic characteristics of the target, such as its reference location (metropolitan area or province), language (we always recommend putting "English"), gender, age, but also some technological variables such as the version of the operating system, the platform (Android, iOs, fixed and portable devices), the model of the device and the telephone operator.

You will also be able to add a number of features that will serve to further segment the audience. The targeting options available are diverse and can be combined to achieve a more accurate target audience. You can choose between the following targeting options.

- **Event targeting.** Use this to reach users interested in events of various kinds on a global or regional scale (holidays, sports, recurring trends, conferences, entertainment, political events).

- **Targeting by behaviors.** You can target the audience based on people's habits, purchase intentions and lifestyles.

- **Targeting by interests.** You can target the audience based on the categories in which they are interested the most.

- **Topics of conversation**. With this option you can target the audience based on specific topics.

- **Similar followers**. You can use this option to reach users with similar interests to a specific profile.

- **Keyword targeting.** You can do this to target searches or users who tweet using the keywords you entered.

- **Movies and TV shows.** You can use this feature to target people interested in movies and TV shows.

In addition, you can reach custom audiences if you have activated the audience measurement tag when setting up the ad group. In this way you may reach those who have already expressed an interest in you through your website, your app or an email list in your possession. These custom segments include so-called Tailored Audience and Flexible Audiences. As this is an introductory book, we will not get into these two advanced types of audience. Just know they exist and they are useless to you.

The local company will also specify whether to retarget users who have viewed previous organic or sponsored tweets, or with whom they have interacted, whether to expand the audience based on characteristics similar to those selected and whether to reach their followers or focus on new people.

Selection of ads and placements

Finally, you have to set up the specific ad. The campaign with click and conversion goal allows you to choose between an already existing tweet or, alternatively, upload a creative to use. You can upload the following types of content.

- Videos
- Images
- GIFs

In addition to that, in the section on the side you can choose the position in which to publish the announcement. This is pretty straightforward and we are sure you will understand it by yourself once you start getting your hands dirty.

After completing the campaign setup process and starting the campaign, you can proceed to create new ad groups as well as new ads for the same group.

Thanks to Twitter ads, companies can get in touch with their audience by establishing conversations of value in order to build loyalty to their brand. Not only is it possible can in fact be addressed to certain people sharing the same interest, within a specific geographical area. This specific feature is particularly appreciated by local businesses like the one used in our example, that can focus their resources to target only people near the physical store.

Now that you have discovered the most important aspects of Twitter for an effective social media marketing strategy, let's dive deeper into another platform that could really help your business get more leads and sales.

Chapter 20

LinkedIn

It is time to discuss a social media that most people never take into consideration when they create a social media marketing strategy. However, in our tests we have discovered that LinkedIn could be a great weapon in your arsenal if you are looking to increase sales, build brand awareness and find new collaborators for your project.

In the next few chapters, we are going to tell you everything you need to know to use LinkedIn in the correct way.

Let's get right into it by looking at how to properly communicate on this social media platform.

Knowing how to best use LinkedIn to develop your online communication is essential if you work in the B2B field. This social network is a goldmine of key contacts in all fields of the professional universe and having a clear idea of how to make the most of it, it means adding very solid leverage to corporate operational marketing.

In reality, LinkedIn is almost always a bit more complex than Facebook when it comes to implementing corporate communication actions or even personal branding. Which if you think about it, it is quite strange, given that it is entirely populated by professionals and therefore it should be more immediate and natural to establish business-oriented contacts.

The point is that on Facebook we think we are entitled to post whatever content goes through our minds. On the other hand, on LinkedIn it is immediately perceived that the quality and adherence of each post to one's professional field must be extremely high. Nobody on LinkedIn would dream of posting a personal photo or a video of a cat falling from a tree.

How then to choose the right actions to take to become protagonists of the LinkedIn universe and attract the attention of potential partners or customers without risking losing credibility?

Here are 5 tips that can allow you to make the most of this social network and improve the quality of your online marketing communication.

Carefully study who you are talking to
Who are you interested in getting in touch with on LinkedIn? Who do you want to reach? If you do not have a proper answer to these questions, it becomes difficult to express a precise and profitable line of action. The first step you must take is to ask yourselves who the recipients of your communication are.

In particular, it is essential to have in mind what the target you aim at expects from you. What interests them the most? What do they need? How can you attract their attention? These are all questions to which you must give a precise answer, in order to publish content that is relevant and in line with the best expectations of your target audienc

Collect valuable content and publish it in a personalized way

In LinkedIn, the most in-depth and thick content wins. Personal or totally emotional communication may perhaps be noticed, but it does not garner a large following in terms of appreciation. Obviously, publishing an engineering treatise on how to remove the casting burrs of a mold will not particularly excite the readers, but if you work in the metallurgical sector, posting an abstract on a study of this kind can help to give a strong impression of competence.

What needs to be done is to never stop collecting valuable content and posting it on a regular basis. Obviously, it is better if these are the result of your own work, but alternatively, content produced by others is also fine. In this case, do not forget to give your magic touch, adding your thoughts and comments. This simple trick will help you show your degree of knowledge of the subject.

Always keep your personal profile up to date

Your personal profile is your LinkedIn business card. Actually, it is even something more than that. It is your online space where you present yourselves as a professional. If you do not take care of it and do not always keep it up to date with the development of your career and your skills, you run the risk that other users of the platform will have an incorrect or inadequate opinion of your professional value.

Furthermore, Google tends to give a good visibility to the LinkedIn profile, when it is completed in all its fields and is equipped with the right keywords. A user could search for your name on Google and find your LinkedIn profile even if he did not search for it intentionally on the social network. For this reason it is essential to take care of your presentation in every detail.

Engage with specific interest groups
On LinkedIn there are many industry groups, which bring together numerous professionals, including renowned ones. While wasting days participating in

the conversations that may arise isn't always profitable, hanging out in the best groups and commenting wisely from time to time can be a recommendable way to easily make new contacts and be noticed.

Posting thick considerations, content of interest, asking relevant questions can also be good ways to show off in a positive way. In particular, knowing how to identify the most interesting conversations and quickly post your contribution can be a good opportunity to attract the interest of the most active people in the group, who are often also appreciated professionals.

Post sponsored content from time to time

Whether you represent a company or want to support your professional image, LinkedIn advertising can be a very effective tool to give you broad and targeted visibility towards your target audience. The costs of advertising on LinkedIn are not prohibitive, so by investing even just a few tens of dollars you can reach people that fit perfectly with your target audience and develop opportunities for new meaningful contacts.

In this case, much attention must be paid to the type of content to be sponsored. It must be useful for those who read them, it must not be too self-referential and must bring real added value to the readers. In addition to that, it must contain a link with what your company or yourselves as professionals can offer to the market. Using advertising in the best possible way to give extra gear to your professional communication activity on this social network.

Keep in mind that LinkedIn, if it is exploited well using all the best operational techniques of social media marketing, can be a goldmine of contacts of great value, especially if you work in the B2B field.

As we have already mentioned in this chapter, having a good profile is key. However, a lot of social media marketers do not know how to optimize it properly. This is why we decided to dedicate a few pages on this important topic.
What to pay more attention to in your LinkedIn account? Which aspects are most important and need to be taken care of? Let's try to answer these questions.

Customize the profile URL

LinkedIn profiles that have a generic alphanumeric URL are difficult to memorize and give the feeling that the user to whom the profile belongs is on LinkedIn by accident or without knowing what he is doing. This gives a feeling of lack of professionalism or lack of motivation. In fact, those who want to contact you will not take you into good consideration if they see a generic link and in some cases will go so far as to think that you are not a good professional. You can simply change your profile URL from the "settings" page. We advise you to do this as soon as you create your account: once it is done, you can forget about it.

Post a nice profile picture

Profiles with a good picture receive far more contact requests than those without a photo. The feeling that profiles without photos give is that those who created it have something to hide, do not feel up to their role or do not take the social network seriously enough. In all three cases it's a bad way to present yourself. Instead, the right way is to choose a serious and self-confident photo, in which you show yourself with the attitude that best represents your professional image.

If you want to take this to the next level, we encourage you to talk to a professional photographer and take some high quality photos.

Include your location

Whether you are looking for a job or are an established professional, letting people know where you are is essential to increase the opportunities to be noticed by a target audience with your contact needs.

Create a clear and effective summary

On LinkedIn, the summary is the short text that explains what you do and your role in the company. Basically, that's what other users see right under the photo and name. An unclear summary considerably reduces the chances of receiving new link proposals or having the ones you sent not being accepted.

To create a powerful summary, you have to try to be creative, but without overdoing it. In fact, people want to feel a little bit of your character, but keep in mind that LinkedIn is not Facebook, so what really matters is what you do and what skills you have.

Participate in relevant and valuable Groups

LinkedIn Groups are the areas where you become part of a community. They are virtual spaces in which it is possible to interact with other professionals in your sector, create stronger relationships, exchange ideas and get noticed. Joining and participating in the life of some valuable groups is a great way to give prestige and visibility to your profile.

Accept connection requests

Many users are reluctant to accept links from strangers on LinkedIn. It's a mistake. In fact, every person on LinkedIn is actually the center of a network of contacts, so if you don't directly care about that person, the connection they have with another user may be useful to you. We remind you that on LinkedIn you will never have to publish private content, but only topics related to your professional sphere, so there is no risk of including people even a little outside your area of competence. Obviously, if you get contacts from people who live in foreign countries, speak an incomprehensible language and have absolutely no point of contact with you, you can avoid the connection. But in all other cases it is better to accept it. In fact, you can eliminate the contact if it turns out to be an annoying person.

Add relevant skills

Skills help to better determine the value of one's professionalism. Although they are almost never what determines the value of a profile, it is always better to enter at least five skills to give your profile a feeling of completeness and clarity.

Use appropriate keywords

LinkedIn profiles are indexed on Google. Furthermore, when you do an internal search in the social network, the system returns precisely those profiles that respond to the search keywords. The keywords that describe you or your company the best and with which you want to be found and identified must be put with the utmost attention in the Summary and in the Description.

Update your profile and add valuable content

A LinkedIn profile is not a static CV. It can and must be updated periodically, introducing new skills and new experiences. In addition, those profiles that have multiple skills will enjoy greater prestige and visibility. Publishing articles within the platform is also an excellent way to improve your profile and make it more effective and valuable. Do not forget to update your profile on a regular basis, it is extremely important.

Chapter 21

Increase Engagement on LinkedIn

How can you generate engagement on LinkedIn? What content do users prefer? These are the questions that LinkedIn has decided to answer through an in-depth study of the habits of its members around the world and investigating the reasons that drive them to use and share content within the platform.

Generating engagement is the goal of every content marketing strategy and to do so you need to know your audience, their habits, their needs and try to communicate with them using their tone and terms. If you want to reach an audience made up of professionals and companies, you cannot fail to consider LinkedIn as your favorite social network where you can share your initiatives and your contents. And in this regard, it is useful to pay particular attention to the internal publishing platform.

All users can take advantage of a dedicated and intuitive space to keep their personal blog without having to leave the platform and with an unprecedented advantage over Facebook. In fact, the published article will not be available only to the personal sphere of user's connections, but will be available to all LinkedIn members in every corner of the globe. If you wish to post the article also on other social accounts, just use the appropriate share feature. In practice, a content published in LinkedIn's editorial platform can be shared anywhere, as if it came from an independent blog. This will allow you to give great visibility to any post and create an extended and multi-channel engagement.

But be careful. In fact, before starting to write or share content within LinkedIn, it should be remembered that it is a platform where subscribers are unlikely to come across selfies and lifestyle pictures, preferring interesting articles over funny posts. In particular, thanks to the analysis of a sample of more than 9,000 users, LinkedIn found that 89% of users prefer news that relate to their work sphere, 86% hope to come across content that contains new or innovative tricks and strategies and 79% prefer to talk about work and business in general terms.

In general, 44% of those who participated in the survey said that they feel more involved by content that is clear, direct and that gets to the point immediately. These people also stated that LinkedIn is their primary source of information to keep up to date when it comes to their professional lives.

Beyond the network of connections that can also be built in order to get in touch with influential personalities to be inspired by, 54% prefer content shared by colleagues and 52% likes content shared by a company or a personal brand.

But how do you generate engagement on LinkedIn by writing and sharing content? 62% of respondents said that they feel more involved when they come across information and training content. Therefore, creating interesting articles that explain how to do things could be a great way to increase engagement and brand awareness.

However, do not forget about the other 48%. In fact, almost half of the people involved in this research, stated that they appreciate reading about the latest news concerning their professional sphere and 40% of those are looking for inspirational articles. Whatever your business is, the only way forward is a thorough study of your target audience to ensure that they are reached by the most suitable content for them exactly when they need it the most. This is why we always remind you to define the target audience before doing anything related to social media marketing. It is fundamentally important to have a clear idea of who you want to reach with your communication, before starting to communicate.

Now that you have understood what people want to read about, it is time to dive a bit deeper into this topic and take a look at some basic tips to write powerful articles on LinkedIn.

New content vs evergreen content

One of the first questions that those who decide to approach the LinkedIn editorial platform for the first time ask themselves is the following one.

What should I publish?

The truth is that there is no rule, it depends on the time available and the goals you intend to achieve. What is certain is that it is always better to opt for quality and potentially interesting content in order to increase your chances of success and, in case you have decided to opt for the revival of a post on your blog, our advice is to change it a little bit. In this way, even if you were to intercept one of your readers, they will not have the impression of being faced with a duplicate content.

Share your articles in groups and other social networks

Once published, your post will be visible to your circle who can recommend and comment on it. However, if you wish to reach more people, you must not underestimate the role of LinkedIn Groups. You should choose the most suitable ones based on the topic of your article. In addition to groups, the article can also be easily shared outside LinkedIn through the buttons of the various social networks or by simply copying and pasting the URL.

Enter a call to action

Let's not forget that any operation carried out outside or inside LinkedIn that is not focused on achieving a specific goal will hardly be helpful for the long term success of your business. Therefore it is better to act in such a way that all your actions respond to a very specific strategy. In this sense, to increase the chances of successful use of the LinkedIn editorial platform, it is always useful to insert at least one call to action, preferably at the end of each article. For example, if it is an article that incorporates a post from your blog, you can insert the link to the original article. This is a particularly suitable technique if your goal is to attract visitors to your site.

Once again, this is why we recommend having a specific social media marketing plan before getting started. Go back to the first few chapters of this book if you need to get this concept fixed in your head.

Now that you know how to set up your profile in the best way and how to create interesting articles, you can start focusing on attracting new clients for your business or personal brand. How do you do it? The next chapter will give you the answer.

Chapter 22

LinkedIn and Clients

As we have seen in previous chapters, LinkedIn is the social network of professionals and given the type and attitude of the users it is in fact the most useful tool for seeking new customers, especially if you work in the B2B niche. In fact, you will hardly come across time wasters that tend to populate other social platforms, like Facebook and Instagram.

However, the very nature of social media requires particular attention in the study of prospects and the strategy to be applied to convert them. Here are some tips that can lead to valuable results by transforming contacts into a goldmine of commercial and business opportunities.

Creating a powerful and trustworthy profile

We have already talked about this, but we feel it is important to remind you one more time. The first step to be successful on LinkedIn is to pay close attention to building your profile, starting with a good photo.

You should choose a cover image that says something about you and, even better, about your work. You should always register using your real name and surname and carefully fill in the fields of your profile to avoid inconsistencies, paying special attention to the compilation of your summary. This, together with the profile picture, the name and the latest experiences will be your business card. Here you should talk about what you are passionate about, what your work consists of and what you want to achieve on LinkedIn. Basically, you need to explain to other users what they can expect from you and what you want from them. Be as clear as possible, it is extremely important to convey the right message.

Make good use of the LinkedIn search engine

LinkedIn offers its users a search engine with a series of filters through which they cannot only search for potential collaborators, but future clients as well. We encourage you to use the traits of your target audience to filter profiles that might be interested in buying your product or service. Once you have done that, you can start connecting with them and build a positive relationship that could convert the prospect into a paying customer. Do not underestimate this strategy as we have gathered good results using it.

Study of prospects and their habits

Once you have drawn up your list of potential customers, you should start the study phase. Try to ask yourself the following questions.

- What activities do they carry out in the company?
- What are their interests in?
- What types of articles do they share the most?

Finding answers to these questions will help you get to know them better. Once you have done this, you can use this knowledge to your advantage when you contact them.

The value of LinkedIn is precisely the possibility of seeing the role that each person has in their company, which allows you to start direct relationships only with people who really care about your product or service.

Do not forget about groups

As you might have noticed, this is a topic that keeps returning in every chapter dedicated to LinkedIn. It is because groups are a very useful tool to connect with potential collaborators and clients.

Many social media marketers make the mistake of choosing the groups to join on the basis of their interests. For example, if they are SEO experts they will look for groups that talk about search engine positioning. However, this is such a big mistake that can literally overthrow your social media marketing plan. In fact, if you proceed like this you will talk to other people that are interested in the same topic as you are, but will not engage with those that actually need your skills or products.

You should subscribe to the same groups your potential customers might be subscribed to, that is the secret.

Direct and personal contact

Once you have identified the people with whom you would like to get in touch, you can proceed to send the connection request. Let's remember, however, that you do not know your prospects personally, so it is better to package a tailor-made message in which you introduce yourselves, without trying to sell you products and services immediately. If you start a dialogue with someone you do not know, first of all you must aim to create interest, in order to develop the relationship in a healthy way.

Once you gain attention and consent, you can start talking about your business and what you have to offer. This is a slow process, but it can yield great results if done consistently and on a regular basis.

Lead generation and advertising

A great way to support the collection of new customers is to use LinkedIn lead generation campaigns. The platform allows you to create advertising campaigns aimed precisely at collecting contacts. LinkedIn ads are extremely effective because the landing page of the advertisement in which users can enter their data is provided by LinkedIn itself. In this way, users do not have to go to an external website, with the risk that some potential leads might not want to do it.

LinkedIn also collects a large part of each user's data directly from those available in its database. In this way, everything is faster and more direct and there is no need to request further data entry that could discourage the potential customer from leaving their personal details and contact methods.

Customer research and lead generation activities usually take a long time before they start yielding appreciable results, so do not be discouraged if things start slow in the beginning.

Chapter 23

Lead generation

At the end of the previous chapter we have discussed lead generation on LinkedIn. In this chapter we would like to expand this concept and look at it from a more general point of view.

We think it is a good idea to start by taking a look at four very important questions you should ask yourself when considering implementing lead generation in your social media marketing strategy.

1. Who do we want to target?

Identifying the target of the actions to be performed is the first step in building an accurate lead generation strategy. You must try to study their characteristics, tastes, behaviors and preferences and draw up a real identity of the typical customer. It might even be useful to give your target audience a name and try to imagine the context in which they live and work in order to approximate a forecast of their behavior. This will give you a much clearer picture of what you can expect.

2. Are you fully aware of the benefits of your company products and services?

The analysis of the strengths and weaknesses of your products and services serves precisely to identify the real benefits that they are able to give to customers and leads. It will be precisely on the basis of these considerations that users will choose whether your company is worthy of their trust or not and it is through the comparison between these and the benefits of the products and services of the competitors that they will decide whether to give you their contact or not.

Therefore, your communication must aim to highlight what distinguishes your product or service from your competitors so that the lead generation strategy can really hit its goal. We feel it could be useful to provide a bonus only for those who have decided to leave their data, immediately repaying them for their trust.

3. Do you have positive testimonials you can leverage?

This question is in some ways connected to the previous one. In fact, users are now much more aware of their role as consumers and are not willing to blindly trust the words of a company. Establishing a solid and lasting relationship with an influencer or pushing your already existing customers to share their experience can be a great way to convince even the most suspicious leads to take action and leave their contact.

4. Do you have a well-defined social media marketing strategy?

The success of a lead generation strategy will depend on all the actions that will be taken, both before and after the acquisition of contacts. For this reason, before starting a lead generation campaign, it is good to have clear in your mind what you want to achieve.

When lead generating, it is important to avoid certain mistakes that can detriment the quality of your work and literally destroy your social media marketing strategy. This is why it is important to know what you are doing in terms of management and organization.

Unfortunately, many people underestimate the effects of improvised management of this online marketing strategy. Our advice is always not to do everything by yourself, but to rely on experts. However, if you find yourselves in the position of doing it alone by choice or because you are on a low budget, then there are some mistakes that must absolutely be avoided in order not to compromise the results.

These are the main mistakes you should avoid.

Not nourishing leads

Contrary to what one might think, most marketers do not consider at all the leads once they have collected them. For lack of time or experience, in fact, there are many companies that do not follow up on the collection of contacts as they should. Instead, you must treasure the contacts you have obtained and take care to respond to everyone. If you do not do that, you will risk throwing away the work of months.

Using landing pages that are way too long

One of the most used tools for lead generation are landing pages and forms. Here there are many mistakes that can be made. First of all, the number of required fields. In fact, you should avoid asking for a thousand details that are not important. You do not want to give the impression you are wasting the potential lead's time.

Too many communications and information after the first contact

Once your leads have been collected, the last thing you need to do is overwhelm them with messages with all the information on all your products and services. It is much better to proceed step by step and increase the communication over time. In fact, too much information and communications all at once could throw users into confusion and even annoy them if you reach out too frequently.

Buying leads

This is a truly unforgivable mistake as well as a useless and harmful shortcut. In the first place, users will not be happy to receive communications from a company they do not even know and the chances of being considered spammers are practically certain. Furthermore, such a practice is also of little use to the company itself. In fact, it is true that in this way you will have avoided some of the work, but what can you do with a bunch of contacts that are almost certainly not on target?

We should also mention that the practice of buying leads is also illegal in some states, so we can only encourage you not to do that.

Think that all leads are created equal

To get the best out of your lead generation strategy, you need to build a tailored communication strategy for each type of potential customer. A newly acquired potential customer will be informed about your products and services, while if you have to contact someone who has already come into contact with your company or personal brand you will opt for a communication that aims to arouse their interest. The best strategy would be to think of a message and a targeted strategy for each level of the funnel in which your potential client is located at every given time.

Chapter 24

How to Create an Effective Landing Page

In this chapter we explain how to create a landing page useful for effective lead generation. In addition to explaining the general characteristics of a good landing page, we highlight the most relevant characteristics of a landing page that allows for excellent results when the goal is to collect leads and contacts from new potential customers.

Let's start by answering a simple question.

What is a landing page?

In general, a landing page is a website page with a specific function. It was created with the aim of achieving a certain goal, which in most cases is the generation of leads. But it can also be used for other purposes: for example, the promotion of a given product in a particular period such as holidays, enrollment in a course or more. Its creation allows to focus the user's attention on the call to action. While the visitor can get distracted on the site due to the presence of so many products and so much different information, in the landing page this does not happen because there is only the necessary information and everything is built with the aim of focusing attention on the call to action.

In particular, if you aim at lead generation, the landing page must have a single purpose: to convince users to leave their personal data. Name and surname, email address, telephone number, company name, professional role are just the most typical contact information that is requested when doing lead generation.

The purpose of lead generation is to get hold of a list of data to be used to create direct and personalized communication with leads.

The main features of an effective landing page are the following.

No distractions

The ideal landing page shouldn't have any distractions. It must be focused exclusively on the reasons why the user must leave his data and must not in any way distract him from this purpose. Any non-essential or irrelevant information and any link other than the CTA is useless and should be deleted.

Immediately highlight the benefits

The unique value proposition is the advantage that the user has in leaving his data. It must be present at the beginning of the landing page. The user who arrives on the landing page must immediately understand what are the benefits he would get in exchange for his contact information and everything he will find later is needed to deepen and confirm these benefits. The headline of the landing page must immediately express these benefits in an attractive way in order to immediately conquer the user's trust.

Use a relevant and expressive image at the beginning

In every effective landing page there should be a beautiful image at the beginning that is able to excite the user. The more a person receives positive emotions, the more he is willing to get involved in what is proposed to him and the less strong his defenses are. It is precisely the images that generate emotions, so the success of a good landing page that wants to collect personal information depends a lot on the reassurance and positive feelings produced by a good image.

Highlight the CTA

The CTA must be placed in an area of the landing page where it can be clearly seen. It usually takes the form of a button, in order to stand out well on the page and entice the user to click it. Possibly some space should be left around it, precisely to focus the visitor's attention in a strong and decisive way. This also means that the CTA cannot be positioned at the bottom of the page, but must be placed at the top, in the immediately visible part of the landing page, to avoid generating disinterest in a user who does not immediately find the call to action he is looking for. If the landing page is particularly long, it is certainly worthwhile to place more than one call to action.

Emotionless CTA text

The CTA must entice the user to click and in general to leave their data. For this purpose it is better to avoid emotionless or not very expressive texts.

For instance, If the benefit you get is to subscribe to a newsletter, rather than saying "Subscribe" the button should show a text like "I want all the updates on the latest news". It is longer, but the message is much more emotional and can be more convincing.

Contrasting colors

Another recommendation to create an effective landing page for lead generation is to use contrasting colors. For example, on a light blue background, a red CTA button stands out very much and draws attention.

If possible, insert a form to collect data

If the purpose of the landing page is to ask users for data, it is advisable to enter the form to be filled directly on the landing page. In this way, the user will not have to travel over several pages to complete the submission of their data and in this way the number of users who will abandon before completing the requested action will be reduced.

Avoid asking for too much personal data

Never give in to the temptation of trying to get too much personal information from users. We get it: the more a person gives you information about themselves the easier it is to categorize them and then send them more targeted and interesting messages. But you have to think that the more data you ask for, the more likely they are to leave the landing page without completing the CTA. It is much better to be satisfied with essential data rather than asking for too much detailed information and greatly reduce the amount of leads collected.

Give guarantees on the correctness of data collection

If a user suspects that their data will not be handled properly they will refuse to give it. A reference to data management and privacy policies, with a link that leads to a page where everything is clarified precisely, serves to reassure the user about the seriousness of the company that is requesting their contact information.

Use the "pre-filled" feature

Whenever possible, it is necessary to create pre-filled fields, in order to facilitate the user in the filling process. For example, if you ask for the market sector in which the company that the user represents operates, it is better to present a drop-down menu listing the main possible fields. This, in addition to speeding up the filling of information, will allow you to collect pre-categorized data and not end up with countless terms that are difficult to aggregate that will make it almost impossible to create well-defined segments.

Short and essential

The user who clearly understands the benefits of leaving their data and who feels trust in those who ask them will not hesitate to enter them. For this purpose, very long and redundant landing pages are not needed. On the contrary, in the case in which you want to lead the user to a fairly impulsive action, brevity and conciseness pay off. A few clear and well-highlighted lines explaining the advantages and opportunities deriving from the granting of personal contact information are enough to convince almost all users. In some cases it may be useful to present the benefits using a bulleted list.

Valuable testimonials

If you have testimonials who can support the value of what is given in exchange for contact data, the effectiveness of the landing page increases significantly. The user feels comforted by a social proof effect. In fact, people tend to consider the behaviors or choices made by a large number of people more valid. This effect increases when the testimonials are well known and appreciated people.

Mobile friendly

Make sure that the landing page is perfectly visible on a mobile device. Much of the traffic will come from smartphones and therefore it is essential that all parts of the landing page are perfectly usable even on a very small display. Also pay attention to the ease of access to the various fields the user has to fill. In fact, the user must never encounter difficulties in entering their data even when using a mobile phone.

Make use of valuable lead magnets

The lead magnet can be defined as the reward that the user receives in exchange for his personal contact details. For example, a white paper, the access to a tutorial, a subscription to a free trial of a service or a product sample. The entire landing page must enhance the advantages of the lead magnet in order to induce the visitor to believe that it is worth giving their email or other identifying information.

Chapter 25

Chatbots and Lead Generation

Besides landing pages, there is another method social media marketers can use to gather leads. We are talking about chatbots.

In fact, they seem to be the new frontier of lead generation. Chatbots are software that provide automatic communication tools to engage with prospects and leads. In practice, thanks to the implementation of features based on artificial intelligence, chatbots can have the so-called Natural Language Processing, which allows the machine to understand, with a very small margin of error, the questions and requests of users who address them, providing coherent answers.

But not only that. The most advanced chatbots are also capable of presenting quotes, showing images, videos, showing a history of a company's activities, illustrating the functionality of a product and more. But these systems are not only capable of providing information. The best designed chatbots are also capable of acquiring information from users who converse with them. And this is precisely where the enormous contribution this tool can make to lead generation lies.

In a dialogue with a prospect, the chatbot can accompany the potential customer along the funnel. In fact, these software can invite users to fill out a form, they can ask for email addresses or other types of contacts. The data received will then be shared with other systems, such as those of marketing automation to grow the list of contacts.

The communication put in place by chatbots can help lead generation thanks to some unique features they have. Let's take a look at them.

Two-way communication

The unique feature of the chatbot is the possibility of putting in place a two-way communication, creating real conversations that do not require to have a real customer care system behind them.

Quick response

To prevent potential customers from getting bored by waiting times, it is necessary to intervene promptly in answering their questions and doubts, otherwise the risk is that they will switch to a competitor or lose interest. A quick response prevents this phenomenon and chatbots can answer immediately.

Data collection

The most advanced chatbots can also collect data, for example by filling an internal database that classifies users based on the level of interest, allowing for a screening of prospects and leads.

Limits of chatbots

The limits that chatbots may have refer to the characteristics of the software, which can be more or less evolved, and to the fact that this tool was just recently created and it is clear that it needs further improvement. For example, it may happen that some terms may not be understood by the chatbot. Another limitation may lie in the use of keywords in a context that the software is unable to recognize. It is also not recommended to use chatbots to communicate promotions and offers, otherwise these messages could be perceived as spam.

Chapter 26

Chatbots and E-commerce

Chatbots can be very useful for increasing sales in e-commerce. In any updated list of today's most impactful technological innovations in the near future of online marketing, chatbots occupy one of the top positions. As we have seen in the previous chapter, chatbots are software capable of establishing a real conversation with users on the web. For example, they can be implemented on corporate sites answering customers questions effectively and pertinently.

At one time these systems were not very efficient due to the large margin of error in understanding user requests. But thanks to the implementation of one of the features of artificial intelligence, Natural

Language Processing, the ability to understand the questions asked has become almost perfect, almost comparable to that of humans. Estimates predict a near future of massive use of chatbots by brands. It has been predicted that by the end 2021 approximately 80% of companies will use these software. If you want to stay ahead of competition you certainly need to implement a chatbot in your social media marketing strategy.

Their use will therefore be increasingly intense and frequent. Just think of all the difficulties that users encounter today when they try to contact a company and you will soon realize the real need for an automated, but intelligent software, capable of answering the questions of consumers, leads and prospects. The waiting times for an answer through the channels available so far, such as telephone, email and so on, are very long.

Chatbots will allow you to solve the problems presented by a user in real time, answering their questions, managing order and in the most sophisticated and advanced cases presenting sales estimates and collecting data. Even e-commerce can derive strong benefits from the integration of chatbots. Here are the main advantages that can derive from the use of chatbots if you have an online store.

Reduction in the number of abandoned carts

One of the most annoying aspects for an e-commerce brand is cart abandonment. About 78% of customers give up on the purchase, leaving a cart full of items without completing the checkout process. The chatbot can reduce this phenomenon by establishing a dialogue with users who are guided in every phase of the sales funnel. The chatbot can make it easier for leads to find what they want. In this sense, the chatbot will be like a personal shopper which will help, support, motivate and therefore facilitate conversion.

Have new sales channels

Users are spending more and more time on mobile devices. Precisely for this reason, new systems are being studied to reach leads on their smartphone, through WhatsApp and Facebook Messenger for example. Rather than just focusing on the company site and waiting for leads to land on it, you can aim to actively reach potential customers. In this case, chatbots can be useful for establishing a dialogue on leads' smartphones and guiding users to the final purchase.

Social media and chatbot integration

Chatbots can also be integrated into social media, to encourage dialogue with brands through these platforms. The phenomenon is already underway on Facebook which has more than 100,000 bots already active on the network. In the future it is expected that through the chatbots integrated with social media it will be possible not only to receive information, but also to carry out real economic transactions and purchases. All of this will become a reality when Facebook will launch its blockchain based project, called DIEM, which will allow in-app real time transactions.

Chapter 27

Chatbots and Facebook Messenger

Using chatbots on Facebook Messenger means giving an important acceleration to your social media marketing strategy. Thanks to these technological tools, companies can open or carry on conversations with followers of the business page without the need to occupy a person's time.

The undeniable advantage of chatbots is that they deliver immediate content to people in an absolutely efficient and, if well planned, effective way.

The downside is that they are not real people. This means that when the user wishes to develop a conversation outside the box, with broader and more in-depth content, the chatbot is no longer able to help them. It should be added that many users do not like relating to a chatbot and find this type of responder very cold and inadequate. The spread of chatbots, however, is leading most people to get used to this kind of relationship with a virtual employee, so at the end of the day it can be said that implementing a chatbot on your page can be a winning choice for your company or personal brand.

The ideal practice is to use chatbots on all those occasions in which communication follows standard and well-predictable content. On the other hand, you should switch to a real conversation in all cases where the chatbot is not able to help the user.

Moreover, you must also think of chatbots as a tool to send messages to users and not just to respond to their contact requests. In this sense they can be a direct marketing tool to be taken into serious consideration.

Here are some tips on how to best use chatbots for marketing on Facebook Messenger.

Automatic replies to frequently asked questions

The most common use of a chatbot is to use it as an automatic responder to the most common and frequent questions that users ask the company. For example, the opening hours, the company telephone number, the address, etc. In all these cases, the bot is able to intercept questions based on the most typical keywords and give satisfactory answers without engaging company employees.

Take orders

Some companies use Facebook Messenger to take orders. For example, it is possible to manage requests for lunches or dinners delivered at home from a restaurant. There are chatbots that allow for the integration of a purchasing platform into the Messenger aoo where users can place the complete order including payment, without the need to speak with a human operator. Some chatbots can also be integrated with the most important e-commerce platforms (for example Spotify) to allow them to make purchases directly within Messenger.

Register users for an event

Both exclusive events in the real world, as well as online events such as webinars, require registration. This is usually done through online forms, which can be integrated into Messenger through special chatbots.

Send messages about events, news and opportunities automatically

Although this type of action can be invasive and annoy some users, if your company has a lot of information and valuable content to give to its customers, Messenger can be a solution. You can program a chatbot to send specific messages, which can help retain users' attention. In addition to that, the company can invite users to participate in particular events, both online and offline, and send messages to remember the date and time after users have signed up.

Offer special discounts and coupons

Very similar to the previous action, in this case the chatbot sends real discount coupons that can be used online or offline, depending on the type of offer that the company has developed.

Launch polls, quizzes and market surveys

Continuously gathering detailed information on customer tastes and interests is essential for companies that want to be successful at social media marketing. There are chatbots that can be integrated into the Messenger app that allow you to create surveys that users can respond to without leaving the chat.

Share new blog posts

Companies that do solid content marketing can implement a chatbot that automatically shares new content posted. In this way, the Messenger app can be transformed into a more immediate and direct alternative to newsletters.

The only warning when using chatbots is not to overdo it. Our suggestion is relatively simple. You should use them to send a few messages, but of high value for the potential customer.

Chapter 28

Social Media Marketing and Artificial Intelligence

In the last few chapters we have talked about the importance of using chatbots and automating some marketing systems. In this chapter, we take a deeper look at the relationship between social media marketing and artificial intelligence.

In fact, an increasingly close relationship is being created between artificial intelligence and web marketing. The trend is to assign to technological systems a multiplicity of functions that are currently performed by people. The benefits can be substantial, because AI is able to process large volumes of information at an enormously higher speed than what humans can handle. Furthermore, they are often systems able to study the contexts in which they operate and implement the most suitable actions to face each new situation.

A question we can ask ourselves is how artificial intelligence can bring benefits to online marketing. Let's make some quick considerations.

What is artificial intelligence?

The term artificial intelligence refers to computer systems capable of making autonomous decisions. They are capable of carrying out a variety of activities that mimic those performed by a human being. Therefore, the criterion of the likelihood between man and machine is one of the parameters that identifies an effective artificial intelligence system.

What online marketing related activities can artificial intelligence systems perform?

The activities that these systems can carry out are numerous and very elaborate, highly evolved in their specifications. These are actions that, as mentioned, mimic human activities. Artificial intelligence is able to make decisions without the supervision of a human being. Precisely for this reason they can carry out complex activities that require the elaboration of a series of quick tasks.

As we have already seen in previous chapters, in online marketing one of the most typical activities of AI systems is that of communicating with a potential customer, understanding the questions asked and answering them in an exhaustive manner. Instead of consulting the FAQ page, a user can for example turn to a chatbot which will clarify doubts and perplexities.

But artificial intelligence systems don't just do this. For example, they can be very useful in making marketing predictions. And in particular, they can probabilistically estimate the behavior of a group of users, and understand in advance the market trend. In particular, thanks to learning machines, the latest generation artificial intelligence software can analyze huge amounts of data on user behavior, while returning forecasts on the effectiveness of a certain campaign in relation to the information already stored. Based on this, intelligent suggestions and targeted offers for consumers can be created.

Men vs artificial intelligence

Therefore, the activities that can largely be carried out by an artificial intelligence system are repetitive ones, which involve careful analysis of a gigantic amount of data. This will leave marketers time to design and test the creative parts of communication and marketing plans. In fact, imagination and sensitivity remain the prerogative of the human mind. Strategic operations must also be implemented by real-life marketers. In fact, only they can understand the details, peculiarities and subtleties of a brand and its market.

It is not beneficial to automate all marketing activities. AI systems must favor and help humans, not replace them, otherwise the sense of the whole marketing system is probably lost.

Furthermore, for an AI system to give its best, a rigorous planning of the activities it must carry out is necessary. When it comes to marketing, it must be included in a strategic framework of actions aimed at supporting the company's business. Therefore, significant competence is required in all the activities that can be carried out to make an effective and truly profitable online marketing strategy.

We can conclude that it is not possible to automate an entire digital marketing plan and that it is fundamental to have a 360° understanding of what needs to be done to turn attention into sales before using chatbots and other artificial intelligence systems.

Chapter 29

Email Marketing

Now that we have discussed the most technological tool there is to do social media marketing, it is time to take a step back and talk about a good old system that year over year proves to be one of the most efficient tools there are to promote a business or personal brand.

We are talking about email marketing and in this chapter we are going to tell you everything you need to know about it.

Email marketing is absolutely necessary in an online marketing strategy. Any operation introduced into the strategic digital marketing plan of a company today must aim at one goal. This goal is the establishment of a relationship as direct and personal as possible with the potential customer.

Email marketing by its very nature establishes a type of one-to-one dialogue between the company and the customer, following up on the marketing communication actions carried out on the web and social media. For this reason, this form of digital marketing is essential in an effective social media marketing strategy, reinforcing or positively concluding the communication flows that the company develops with its audience.

So let's see the 3 main reasons why a social media marketing strategy cannot be considered complete if it does not include email marketing.

Everyone uses email and your company or personal brand should to

The importance of email marketing depends on three main factors.

1. Everyone has at least one email address and uses it regularly.

2. The e-mail box is a suitable channel for direct, personal and at the same time discreet communication with paying clients and potential customers. The winning character of this communication channel lies precisely in its non invasive communication.

3. The third point in favor of email marketing derives from the first two and refers to user expectations. In fact, customers expect to receive emails from companies they like and are interested in. If your personal brand or online business does not make use of email marketing, you are leaving money on the table.

Great value and variety of content conveyed with emails

Emails can include extremely varied content. From simple text messages to real web mini-sites, to the inclusion of videos and multimedia content of all kinds. You can send newsletters that have the form of real online magazines, or extremely personalized and targeted emails in which a single topic that interests the customer is discussed.

The graphics and visual quality of emails today is very sophisticated and companies that know how to create very rich and engaging emails are very likely to win the trust and attention of customers and potential clients.

Targeted messages can be sent to each user

Thanks to the latest generation email marketing software (such as ActiveCampaign, Sendinblue, MailChimp, MailUp and Aweber) it is possible to detect user behavior every time they receive an email. You can find out if they have opened it and if they have clicked on the links you have put in the email.

The most sophisticated software allows you to create email marketing automation plans. These allow you to schedule emails to be sent based on user behavior in relation to the emails they have already received. In practice, the system detects which emails each user of the mailing list appreciates most, evaluating the open rate of every single email.

In this way it is possible to understand which topics interest each user the most and schedule emails to be sent closer to their real interests. The result is obvious: users become increasingly interested and involved in the contents of the emails received. Over time, users will find more and more stimulating opportunities to buy products that satisfy their real desires and make purchases.

It is also possible to link the sending of a specific email to the actions performed by a user on the company website, for example when they have viewed a product page or added a product to the cart. For instance, if a user has visited a product page on the company's e-commerce site, it is possible to program the automatic sending of an email with an article or video that explains the ways to best use that product. Or alternatively, you can automatically send an email that offers a particular purchase opportunity, for example a discount if they buy the product within 24 hours.

In this way, over time, users will receive increasingly stimulating and engaging messages that will lead them to become increasingly interested in the company and its products, greatly increasing the likelihood of them making a purchase.

How much can a company that carries out email marketing campaigns and has a good customer mailing list earn? Whether sales are made through an e-commerce site or in situations where messages are sent only to create interest in the company or products, email-based digital marketing campaigns are extremely profitable.

The fundamental questions that must be asked when the company evaluates the launch of a long term email marketing campaign are the following.

What is the return on investment that can be expected? How much does a campaign of this kind yield in economic terms? What aspects and key performance indicators must be considered to correctly evaluate this type of digital marketing strategy?

The parameters (KPIs) to consider

In chapter 7, we have discussed the importance of measuring KPI and we have given clear directions on which need to be considered. When it comes to email marketing, there are a few small changes to be made to that list.

When sending an email to the mailing list, you must take into account the following KPIs.

- The size of the mailing list. This is represented by the total number of emails you send.

- The percentage of active email addresses present in the mailing list and corresponding to users who are really in target in respect to the company's reference market.

- The open rate (OR). This is the amount of emails that are opened in relation to those sent.

- The amount of clicks on the call to action present in the email compared to the total number of emails sent. This is also known as the click-through rate or CTR.

These quantitative and perfectly measurable parameters must also be associated with qualitative aspects. You should always consider the following points.

- How interesting and stimulating is the topic of the email?
- How much does the email subject tempt the user to open it?
- Does the email have a good aesthetic and graphic?
- Is the content written in a clear, direct and engaging way?

These aspects essentially refer to the quality of the emails that are created and sent. The higher the quality of a message, the greater the likelihood that it will be opened by those who received it and that it will arouse interest in clicking on the call to action. Most campaigns that do not achieve consistent results have a flaw in the quality of the messages, which are often written by people who are not specialized or competent in email marketing and content marketing, with the effect of greatly reducing the success of the campaign.

The landing page

Another factor must be considered and this is the email landing page. This is the web page to which a user is directed when they click on the call to action inserted in the email. It is usually a page on the business website, but it can also be created ad hoc on other specific platforms.

The quality of the landing page is another success factor. In fact, if the user finds valid content on the landing page and in line with what interested them in the email, the likelihood of completing the expected action increases significantly.

Email marketing and sales

An email can generate many reactions in a user, but obviously the most profitable emails are those that immediately translate into a purchase. Companies that have an e-commerce site can turn emails into immediate sales opportunities. In this case, for each email that offers particular purchase opportunities, the revenue obtained in terms of sales conversions can be calculated immediately and exactly.

In cases where you do not have an e-commerce site, the calculation of the profitability of an email marketing plan is obviously less accurate, but there may be methods that allow you to verify the effectiveness and profitability of an email.

For example, if the goal is to attract customers to a store, you can offer coupons, the opportunity to receive gadgets or even invite them to an exclusive event in which they can participate by showing the invitation received via email. Measuring the amount of people who answered the call to action in this way becomes very easy. Obviously, you will then have to understand how much each of these people is worth in terms of purchases actually made at the point of sale.

How to calculate the revenues generated by an email marketing campaign

How can you calculate the value of an email marketing campaign? The simplest and most direct way is to consider the sales of an e-commerce site.

The scenario is that of a company that sells products through an electronic business platform and has collected a good amount of email addresses. These email addresses are as much as possible in target with the target audience.

To this mailing list, send a well-designed email with content that induces the potential customer to make a purchase, perhaps offering a discount, the cancellation of shipping costs, a gift that will be received upon delivery of the product, etc. The call to action, which corresponds to a button or a link allowing the user to better discover the product and the purchase proposal, leads to a well-designed landing page, which in some exceptional cases can also be the same product page on the e-commerce site, where the customer can complete the conversion by making the purchase.

In this context, which normally corresponds to the standard one of a professionally designed e-commerce sales-oriented email marketing campaign, it is possible to easily calculate the revenues and therefore the earnings on each email sent.

To calculate the results, some parameters must be defined. You should always take these parameters into consideration when crafting an email marketing strategy.

- **Email CTR**. This refers to how many users click on the call to action.

- **Landing page conversion rate.** This refers to how many users who visit the landing page make a purchase.

- **Average value of the purchase made**. This refers to the average expense that a user makes when making the purchase (if a specific product is proposed, this is the cost of the product)

- **Profit margin that the company has on the product.** This is what remains for the company as a profit on each sale, without yet considering the cost of the email marketing campaign.

The CTR standards can be obtained from many authoritative studies carried out on a very high number of email marketing campaigns. Among the most valid was the recent ones carried out by MailChimp, Barilliance, Marketing Insider Group, and Instapage. Based on these analyzes, a CTR between 2.5% and 3.0% can be considered good.

As for the landing page conversion rate, the Unbounce study is very reliable, which fixes it at around 4%. It must be said, however, that in highly effective campaigns where the purchase advantage is very high, it is acceptable to have a conversion rate that can go up to 10% in some lucky cases.

Based on these parameters it is possible to have an accurate picture of the revenues and earnings generated by a good email marketing campaign.

Cost and income ratio and return on investment

The costs of an email marketing campaign are usually quite low. They amount on average to 500 and 1,500 dollars per month depending on the complexity of the segmentation. On average, email marketing campaigns send between 4 and 10 emails per month to each user of the mailing list.

Normally the operational management costs do not vary too much depending on the size of the mailing list, while the costs of using the email marketing software may vary in this sense. Some platforms calculate the cost of using the application according to the number of contacts in the list, while others in relation to the number of emails sent monthly.

In this sense, when you have a mailing list of less than 5,000 users, it may not be convenient to invest in agencies or professionals specialized in email marketing, capable of maximizing the results and the revenues of a campaign. In this case, to have a better return on investment, it is better to eventually follow a training course and manage the sending of emails internally, mostly in the form of newsletters or emails with more generic sales proposals.

When the number of contacts in the mailing list exceeds 5,000 people, then the choice of investing in an agency or professionals specialized in email marketing becomes a winner. In fact, these digital marketers will be able to obtain the best results from each email and will be able to optimize every step of the campaign, in order to maximize revenues and earnings. These professionals will be able to transform a good mailing list into a significant source of income which, moreover, will help the company to maintain constant and appreciated contact with its leads and paying customers.

Chapter 30

15 Email Marketing Tips

Email marketing can bring extraordinary results in terms of return on investment. An analysis conducted by Campaign Monitor reveals that the use of the email channel can lead to a return on investment of up to 4,400%. In other words, for every dollar invested you can get up to 44 dollars. Obviously, the indispensable condition is that the design of the emails and the management of the entire process are carried out in the best possible way.

In this chapter we give you 10 practical tips you can implement today to maximize the results of your email marketing strategy.

1. Segment the mailing list

A mailing list is made up of a set of email addresses of which some specific information about the owner is often known. If the emails come from well-designed lead generation campaigns, perhaps you know the name and surname of the user, the city in which they live, age, gender and phone number. These data allow to segment the mailing list on the basis of specific groups of users to whom it is possible to send different and more targeted contents and proposals.

Emails that reach all users of an email marketing campaign without distinction lose effectiveness, because they will only be of interest to a small part of the subscribers to the mailing list. In general, email marketing campaigns that take advantage of mailing list segmentation increase the email open rate by 203%.

2. Check the quality of the mailing list

Most of the user data owned by companies is unreliable or out of date. A rather disturbing reality, which concerns at least 60% of the marketing departments of companies. Having more precise information about the users to whom messages are sent is essential if you want to improve the result of marketing campaigns. Without this information, it is impossible to make good segmentation of the mailing list and therefore the outcome of email marketing campaigns is compromised.

There are many ways to get deeper insights into your customers and leads. Sometimes the same email marketing software allows you to insert questionnaires and surveys in emails and they detect and record the actions of users regarding the messages sent. A user who regularly opens messages on a certain topic is probably also interested in receiving relevant products. On the other hand, every time they receive emails on another topic, they immediately delete them without even opening them.

Most software are able to associate each user with their choices and use them to enrich the information on their account and therefore to better target the contents to be sent over time.

3. Use marketing automation

When you have a very large mailing list, it is difficult to send well-differentiated emails based on the various segments into which users have been divided without using specific technological tools.

The best software offers email marketing automation technologies that allow you to schedule the mailings dynamically, defining email plans to be sent automatically to all users who have performed a certain action, and have reacted in a certain way to the emails received previously.

In general, the use of email marketing automation techniques increases revenues by 320% compared to a campaign that does not use automation.

4. Correctly formatting your emails

Users open at least 53% of emails received using a mobile phone or a tablet. On these devices, however, the formatting of the emails is different from how it appears on a computer screen. For this reason, you must pay the utmost attention to creating perfectly responsive formatting also optimized to be viewed on mobile devices. Fortunately, most email marketing software today are able to provide pre-configured templates to be viewed on smartphones and tablets. However, it is always advisable to carry out preliminary tests to verify that the aesthetic and communicative effect obtained on the small screen of a mobile phone is satisfactory.

5. Personalize the emails

Each user likes to perceive that whoever sends an email is speaking specifically to them and not to all the public without distinction. One of the fundamental rules in creating truly effective emails is personalization, which helps reduce the distance between the recipient of the email and the company.

"Good morning James, today is your birthday and to celebrate we want to give you an exclusive gift! If you buy any product on our site today, we will give you an item of your choice worth 10 dollars". Such a message hits the mark and highlights the attention that the company pays to each of its customers as a person and not just as a number on a mailing list.

In general, personalized emails allow you to increase by 6 times the purchase conversions that non-personalized emails can generate. We encourage you to go the extra mile and produce high quality and personalized emails, they will certainly yield amazing results over time.

6. Beware of calls to action

When you send a message to a user, you must explicitly tell them what you want them to do. This happens in the call to action (CTA), which must be present in every email. From the company's point of view, the CTA is often the primary reason why the email is being sent. "Buy the product", "register for the seminar", "take advantage of the discount", "register for the event", etc. are some possible examples of CTAs.

The problem is that there is often a tendency to abuse CTAs, ending up with too many in the same message. There are cases where this can make sense, such as when presenting a list of products that are currently on sale. But in most cases it is best to enter no more than one or two CTAs per email. In fact, as many user behavior analyzes have found, emails with a single CTA greatly increase click-through rates. WordStream even notes that the increase is 371% compared to messages that contain too many calls to action.

7. Always allow users to unsubscribe

The legislation for sending marketing emails requires the message to contain a link that allows the user to unsubscribe automatically. The GDPR (General Data Protection Regulation) makes it mandatory for those who send emails to immediately unsubscribe a user from a mailing list if the user requests it.

Sending emails without giving users the possibility to unsubscribe as well as being incorrect and disrespectful to users is also dangerous, because some users could report the company to the Privacy Guarantor.

8. Choose the words of the email carefully to avoid being considered spam

Almost all email box providers now offer spam filters that identify, based on particular algorithms, which messages are advertising or annoying and which ones have a good content value. This happens based on a number of different parameters, one of which is precisely the detection of keywords typical of spam emails. These words must be avoided or otherwise used with great caution.

Although obviously it is not certain that the inclusion of these words will immediately cause the email to be classified as spam here are the terms that should be used as little as possible.

- **Offer indicators.** Free, offer, promotion, gift, loan.

- **Urgency indicators.** Limited time, hurry, now.

- **Call to action explicitly linked to orders or money.** Ask for a quote, buy now, order now.

- **Trivial teasers.** You won't believe your eyes, the secret nobody wants to let you know.

9. Avoid sending emails to accounts that have not subscribed to the mailing list

Companies often buy email lists from agencies that offer pre-made lists of potential customers based on specific niches. This is almost always a mistake. First of all the users have not authorized the company to send them emails, with the effect that the unsubscribe rate will be very high and this will make the email service providers suspicious. Furthermore, a user who has not expressed an explicit interest will almost always find the messages sent not very stimulating and will tend not to open them, making the mailings useless and penalizing the campaign.

The best solution is to invest in valid lead generation campaigns, with which you can obtain well-profiled email addresses of potential customers who are truly interested in the company's services and products. This is why we have dedicated different chapters to lead generation techniques. We encourage you to follow our recommendation.

10. Pay maximum attention to the email subject

35% of people who receive an email decide to open it only based on what they find written in the subject. If this is interesting and knows how to intrigue users, then the chances of the email being opened become very high. Otherwise, the opening rate is drastically reduced even if the email may contain valuable content.

A good subject should be incisive and capable of hinting at the contents of the email.

If you have no idea how to write a powerful subject for your emails, do not worry. The next few pages will teach you how to do that.

Creating an effective and incisive subject, suitable for the type of audience you intend to reach or the type of communication you want to pursue, can really make the difference between a successful and a failed email marketing strategy. Here are 5 tips to create engaging subjects for your emails.

1. Write in a clear and concise way

Being mysterious can be a good strategy in social media marketing, but it almost never works when it comes to emails. Users are now used to receiving all kinds of emails from spammers with incredible promises, mysterious announcements or bombastic statements. These types of messages are now immediately perceived as unwelcome, if not dangerous, and are usually thrown away before being opened, when not reported as spam. To avoid this type of problem, the email subject must be written clearly without ambiguity.

2. The subject must communicate a sense of urgency

What could convince the recipient of an email to open the message better than a limited opportunity in time? The subject must trigger a spring in the user's mind that pushes them to act so as not to miss an otherwise unrepeatable opportunity. You can communicate all this by defining a time limit within which the proposal contained in the email is valid, highlighting precise dates in which a certain action can be taken.

However, be aware of the list of terms you should avoid using. You can find it just a few pages back.

3. Short and simple

When you think about the subject of an email, you must follow the saying "Less is more". The vocabulary and phrasing to use must be simple, because emails are often read in conditions in which the user is not very attentive and focused, especially when consulting the mail with devices such as mobile phones and tablets.

Furthermore, the text must be extremely short and concise. It should not be forgotten, in fact, that a subject that is too long will be cut, especially when the email is displayed on a mobile phone. In general, you should try to keep it between 25 and 30 characters and in any case not to exceed 50. In general, emails with a higher open rate are those with a subject that does not exceed 30 characters.

4. Consider when to use emojis

Technically speaking, it is possible to use emojis in the subject of an email. However, this is a decision that must be taken with caution and attention. Not all recipients, in fact, are sensitive to "smilies" and graphic symbols and depending on the type of company it can even be perceived as not professional.

Therefore, you have to study the habits and characteristics of your target audience and decide accordingly. You should always avoid the risk of sending a message that is perceived as not serious or valuable. If the recipients are very young then emojis are welcome. But if you are sending emails to insurance and banking professionals, emojis are probably not particularly appropriate.

5. Numbers, questions and calls to action always work

Numbers can be a great way to present the content of an email. In fact, it is as if they serve as a guide for the user who can already get an idea of what awaits them.

Questions can also be a great gimmick, especially when used in a sentence that expresses a sense of urgency.

Finally, inserting a call to action already within the subject of an email can be an excellent method as they present the user what is the next move to be made.

Chapter 31

Email Marketing and Videos

Using videos in email marketing is a good way to send truly interesting messages with content that catches the attention and manages to engage users. As a matter of fact, videos are the type of content that web users like the most right now. This is first of all confirmed by the use of social media statistics, which show how videos are the most popular type of post by subscribers.

The rapid growth of TikTok, a social media based on the publication of short videos, confirms this trend, while YouTube remains firmly in the top ten positions of the most visited sites on the entire web.

Inserting videos into emails can then be an effective communication technique to make messages richer and more stimulating. A video can significantly increase the interest aroused by the proposed content, convincing the user to follow the proposed call to action.

How to include videos in emails

Most email marketing software offers the ability to insert videos into emails. In some cases, embedding can also be done with elegant graphics, which helps to raise the aesthetic quality of emails.

However, it should be noted that in general, when including a video in an email, it is always advisable to add explanatory text. Not all users are willing to watch the video, so without the text they would not receive any messages. Obviously, the text must be very concise and summarize the content of the video or induce people to enjoy the video. For example, if the video is an excerpt from a fashion show, the text could sound something like this. "Discover the latest fashion proposals that are trendy for this summer! Watch the video now!".

If you do not include the video directly into the email because it may be too long or too heavy, you can place it inside a landing page. In this case, the email can encourage users to watch the video on the dedicated external page. There are several cases in which a video can really make a difference in the content of an email and turn an email marketing campaign into a success, with a higher than average click-through rate (CTR). Here are some tips on how to do email marketing making the most out of videos.

Videos with company representatives summarizing the content of the email

One of the typical problems with emails is having to be extremely concise in the text, otherwise the reader will not reach the end of the message. This requires a great ability to synthesize, but at the same time it often prevents marketers from being sufficiently clear and explanatory about what they want to express. The effect is that emails often become too emotional, eventually failing to hit the mark or to provide comprehensive information.

In other cases, when you really can't help but explain the content in more detail, the email is too verbose and boring, with the effect of not being read entirely by most recipients or even being thrown away immediately after opening. To solve these problems, you can include a video in the email in which a person from the company briefly explains the content of the email. In this way, two results are obtained. The first is that the email appears more personal and humanized, because a person who speaks directly to the users creates an emotional connection with them. The second result is that it is possible to expose the content in a warmer and broader way without tiring the user.

Of course, the video must be short. It is much better if it does not exceed one minute. You can make videos that are a little longer only if the proposed theme is actually very exciting and particular.

Testimonial videos

It is not always easy to convince your customers or other people who appreciate the company and its products or services to share their feedback. Even more difficult is persuading them to record a video and obtain permission to use it for corporate marketing communication. However, if you can produce this kind of video, for example in exchange for some gadgets or bonuses, it is a good tactic to include these videos in your emails.

Presenting a product and supporting it with a video testimony makes your communication much more credible. Even more effective is to place testimonials as the subject of the email. For example: "What our customers think of our ties" or "Do you agree with what our customers think of us?". This second way of formulating the subject is more risky because it directly questions the opinion of the user of the email, but it is certainly very engaging.

Video tutorial

Explaining how a product is best used or how to best benefit from a service is often a great way to encourage a purchase. This type of content rarely is appropriate to the direct and immediate communication typical of emails, but if you create a useful and incisive video tutorial you can send it with good results. For example, you can show how to spread a cream to get the best benefits or produce a video in which a particular makeup is proposed. The user will immediately perceive the product presented as something immediately usable and will emotionally feel the benefits of it.

Furthermore, if the video contains valid suggestions on how to make the most of the product for a certain purpose or in general on how to do something, the recipient of the email will increase the esteem and trust in the company.

Video for customer service

In a customer care context, when sending emails that respond to problems expressed by customers, it can be a winning choice to give the answer through a video in which the customer service employee speaks. In this way, the customer will have the feeling of truly receiving a personalized message and of having paid greater attention to their requests. In addition, a video message is often easier to understand than a written text. In many cases, this greater clarity will help resolve disputes or reduce customer dissatisfaction.

Enter a video presentation of the company or products at the end of the email

Even if you send an email with content centered around text, you can complete the email with a video that presents the company and its products in an institutional way. Closing the email with a video presenting the latest products, proposing a tour of the company or showcasing other situations regarding the company or products is a great way to increase the overall value of the message.

Users who decide to watch the video will have an even more positive opinion of the company and what it offers to the market.

Do not underestimate the power of including videos in your emails. It might be the decisive tactic that revolutionize your entire business.

Chapter 32

Google Ads

We are entering the final chapters of this book and we would like to take some time to talk about a powerful marketing tool at your disposal to increase the number of leads and sales. We are talking about Google advertising, or Google Ads in short.

From the point of view of a company or personal brand it is a way to automatically publish your advertisement on a large number of sites sharing similar characteristics and topics. In this way the company can reach a homogeneous and targeted audience using many channels, but without bothering to contact all the publishers one by one to agree on the publication of the ad.

Used in the most valid way Google AdSense is one of the most effective and pervasive online advertising models. So let's see in summary what the most salient features of this form of advertising on the web are.

The types of Google AdWords campaigns

There are therefore two possible types of search engine campaigns regarding the places where Google can show advertisements to its users: search network campaigns and display network campaigns.

Search Network Campaign

This type of campaign displays ads at the top of search results pages, called SERPs. These are text-only ads that are created through Google AdWords.

Display network campaign

On the other hand, it is possible to show your advertising on similar sites that are partners of Google. In this case, the ad may be presented in the form of banners with the advantage of having a potentially more attractive visual appearance than simple text.

What is Google AdSense?

AdWords advertisers can choose to show their ads on partner sites that are part of the circuit. We can look at the definition of Adsense from the perspective of affiliate sites. In fact, AdSense is the tool that allows partner sites to display advertisements from AdWords advertisers, earning based on the clicks that the ads receive. When the user clicks on the ad, they will be redirected to a page of the company website or to a landing page.

What kind of users can be reached through AdSense?

For example, through AdSense it is possible to reach users with a particular geolocation. This is particularly useful for physical stores, which must be able to reach users who live in a specific city. Additionally, advertisers' ads are shown on relevant sites. For example, the announcement for the sale of a fishing rod could be shown on a blog that deals with hunting and fishing. This will make it easier to reach users with specific interests.

Properly managing AdSense is not easy if you want to have effective results and not waste your investment in advertising in views and clicks that are not well targeted. In general, all forms of traditional online advertising today AdWords has the advantage of placing banners in a dynamic and contextual way. In fact, it takes into account the specificities of the site and the web pages on which the ad is published. In this way it is possible to intercept those people who are actually interested in the content of the ad, because this is consistent and similar to the contents of the page on which it is located.

To create this perfect congruence of the ad with the contents of the sites in which it is published, a number of parameters that can be managed through the AdWords interface must be set correctly. If this work is done well, great results can be achieved, especially in terms of brand awareness and sales.

Chapter 33

Google Ads or Facebook Ads?

What is the best platform for online advertising? This is the question of the moment in the field of digital marketing. And in fact, when you intend to allocate a portion of the budget to paid advertising, choosing the right platform is crucial for the success of your campaigns. Facebook Ads and Google Ads are the most important online advertising channels in the US. However, these have different characteristics, and they allow you to reach different audiences.

Will users look for us or will we look for them?

One of the first points to be resolved, before implementing an advertising strategy, refers to the ways in which the company will be reached by online users: will the user be looking for it or will the company find potential customers? In fact, Facebook and Google are advertising arenas based on profoundly different assumptions. Facebook is a social network that users connect to to stay in touch with friends and relatives and to cultivate their interests. Usually the subscribers to the social network are not active in searching for contents, but they find the contents that other users publish in their news feed in a more or less passive way. The content that is displayed depends on the activity of the friends with whom they are in contact with. In fact, it is the Facebook algorithm that decides what to show users.

Instead, Google is a search engine. Users actively turn to it to search for what is of interest to them, resolve doubts and satisfy curiosity.
It is fundamental to keep this difference in mind when elaborating a paid advertising strategy.

Different phases of the buyer's journey
The difference between the two platforms also lies in the buyer's journey phase, which is the set of

sequential actions performed by a user before making a purchase. On Facebook, people who are at the top of the funnel can be easily reached. These are users who still do not even know they are interested in the company's products. For instance, if you have to promote a photography course, you can include photography among the interests of users when creating your audience on Facebook Business Manager. All users who have this interest will find the company's advertisement and will be able to become aware of its specific offer. Some of these users will then begin to take the company into consideration when deciding to purchase a product of that type. Others will begin to think that the product can actually respond to some specific need and will begin to evaluate it.

On Google Ads, on the other hand, through the Search Network, you can reach users who have a clearer idea of what they want. These people find themselves at a lower level of the funnel.

Which is better?

If you ask yourself the question "Is it better to use Google Ads or Facebook Ads?", the answer is simple: it depends. You must consider the goals of the campaign, the way in which the buyer persona will probably search or find your company on the internet and what level of the sales funnel you intend to work on.

Often it is better to act on both advertising arenas to cover all types of possible customers and to be found on both channels, which intercept different phases of the same possible customer.

Defining an effective online advertising plan is anything but trivial. The aspects to be evaluated are numerous and refer both to the specifics of the products and the company, and to the characteristics of the ideal customer to whom the product is addressed. Designing and managing an advertising campaign in the best possible way means not only having a significant return on investment in the short term, but laying the foundations for a more solid relationship with customers in the long term as well. As you should understand by now, the only way to determine which advertising platform works better for your business is to test them extensively. Only by trying new things and refining your strategies you will be able to define a complete social media marketing plan that works and turns leads into customers. When experimenting with paid traffic, our suggestion is to start slow and build the budget up over time. In this way, you will be able to see what works and what needs to be corrected, without risking losing too much money.

Keep testing and we are sure you will discover what type of advertising works best for your company or personal brand.

Conclusion

Congratulations on making it to the very end of this book, it has been a great journey.

We hope you were able to find valuable information to monetize the online presence of your company or personal brand. We have tried our best to give you every tool and strategy you might need to turn your social media pages and company website into money making machines.

Now it is on you to put in practice what you have learned. Because remember that understanding a concept and making it work for you are two totally different things and as an entrepreneur or influencer you should always be willing to take the risk to try and test new strategies.

We are sure that if you commit to seriously working on your social media marketing strategy, you will be well ahead of competition. After all, it is not a secret that most businesses have a superficial approach when it comes to their online presence. Doing things differently will certainly put you miles ahead of them and will give you an unfair advantage in the long run.

If you find valuable information in this book, we kindly encourage you to share it with other people that might be interested in digital marketing. Sharing is caring, never forget that.

We hope you enjoyed this book and we wish you great success!